LOWESTOFT TRAMWAYS

David Mackley

Series editor Robert J Harley

MP Middleton Press

Cover Picture:
Fifteen open top double deck trams, built in 1903/4, were the mainstay of tram services in Lowestoft until closure in 1931. These cars remained essentially unaltered throughout their service lives. Car 5 is seen here in its twilight years on 21st April 1929 at 6.22 pm and outside the Maypole stores in Station Square. (Dr H.Nicol/ National Tramway Museum)

Rear Cover:
Lowestoft car 14 is undergoing its second restoration at the East Anglia Transport Museum, since its saloon was rescued in 1962. The first (cosmetic) reconstruction was largely complete by about 1970, when it was painted in an unlined and mostly unlettered livery. (A.Howard)

A serious start on a total structural rebuild into operating condition was made in 2003. By January 2010, the semblance of a tram was taking shape. (Author)

Cover colours: These reflect the livery of Lowestoft Corporation Tramways.

Details of the East Anglia Transport Museum's opening times and special events can be seen at www.eatm.org.uk

Published April 2010

ISBN 978 1 906008 74 1

© Middleton Press, 2010

Design Deborah Esher

Published by
    Middleton Press
    Easebourne Lane
    Midhurst
    West Sussex
    GU29 9AZ
Tel: 01730 813169
Fax: 01730 812601
Email: info@middletonpress.co.uk
www.middletonpress.co.uk

Printed in the United Kingdom by Henry Ling Limited, at the Dorset Press, Dorchester, DT1 1HD

CONTENTS

Rotterdam Road	1	The Bridge	45	Tramway people	88
Denmark Road	3	Pier Terrace	57	High Days & Holidays	94
London Road North	5	London Road South	67	Permanent Way	100
High Street	16	Pakefield	76	Rolling Stock	102
Yarmouth Road	23	Rotterdam Road Depot	81	Finale	117
Station Square	33	Power Generation	84		

INTRODUCTION AND ACKNOWLEDGEMENTS

The Lowestoft tramways were distinctive in a number of ways. Arguably they had the most elaborately appointed fleet of electric cars in East Anglia. The line crossed a swing bridge on which the overhead power lines moved with that bridge. Passage of trams was controlled by railway type signals. It was the most easterly tramway in the British Isles. It was also the smallest electric tramway in East Anglia and had only a single route. For this latter reason, assembling 120 photographs of it has been no easy task. Some parts were photographed in profusion, so our pictorial tour proceeds almost yard by yard in the harbour area. Pictures of cars at the northern extremity of the line, on the other hand, have totally eluded the author. Some pictures of less than perfect quality have been included to illustrate particular aspects.

I am indebted to organisations and individuals who have made this book a possibility. The Suffolk Record Office, Lowestoft Branch, provided access to Lowestoft Tramways Committee minutes and other records. They also cleared the way for the use of a number of images in this book; notably from the Christopher Wilson and Lowestoft Borough collections. A wealth of historical material, of which this volume can only scratch the surface, was unearthed through the services of the National Archives at Kew. The Bodleian Library at Oxford provided extracts from Ordnance Survey maps from the 1904 and 1927 surveys, as indicated.

Peter Larter was particularly helpful in making connections with sources of photographs and in preparing quality prints. Alan Brotchie kindly made available pictures from the late Jack Herd's collection, as well as from his own. Other pictorial contributions are acknowledged in the text; every effort being made to attribute them as accurately as possible with sincere apologies offered where any unintended error or discourtesy has occurred. Assistance in a range of forms was also provided by M. Andrews, C. Brooks, F. Dunham, D. Friston, J. Holmes, D. Jones, M. Lawrence, I. Robb and B Ward. My wife, Kathrine, typed a legible script from my spidery draft.

Particular mention should be made of the late A.V. (Dick) Bird who loved the Lowestoft trams as a boy and gathered together material relating to the tramways (including photographs) in the 1960s. He ensured the survival of the body of car 14 and founded the East Anglia Transport Museum, where 14 could run again. The Museum has encouraged the production of this book from the very beginning and made their own archives available.

Whilst this volume does not purport to be a full history, the author has incorporated into the text and maps some of the fruits of his own researches which, in certain instances, amend the record as set out in earlier histories. The author does not profess to have had the last word on the subject, however, and is very open to hearing of further information or material.

There was a familial feel to the small Lowestoft tramway system and this carried over to the municipal bus services until their sad demise in 1977. As in so many towns, the end of council-run transport meant the loss of a symbol of local identity in the street scene. This book is dedicated to the crews, engineers, support staff, managers and local politicians who kept wheels turning for three generations.

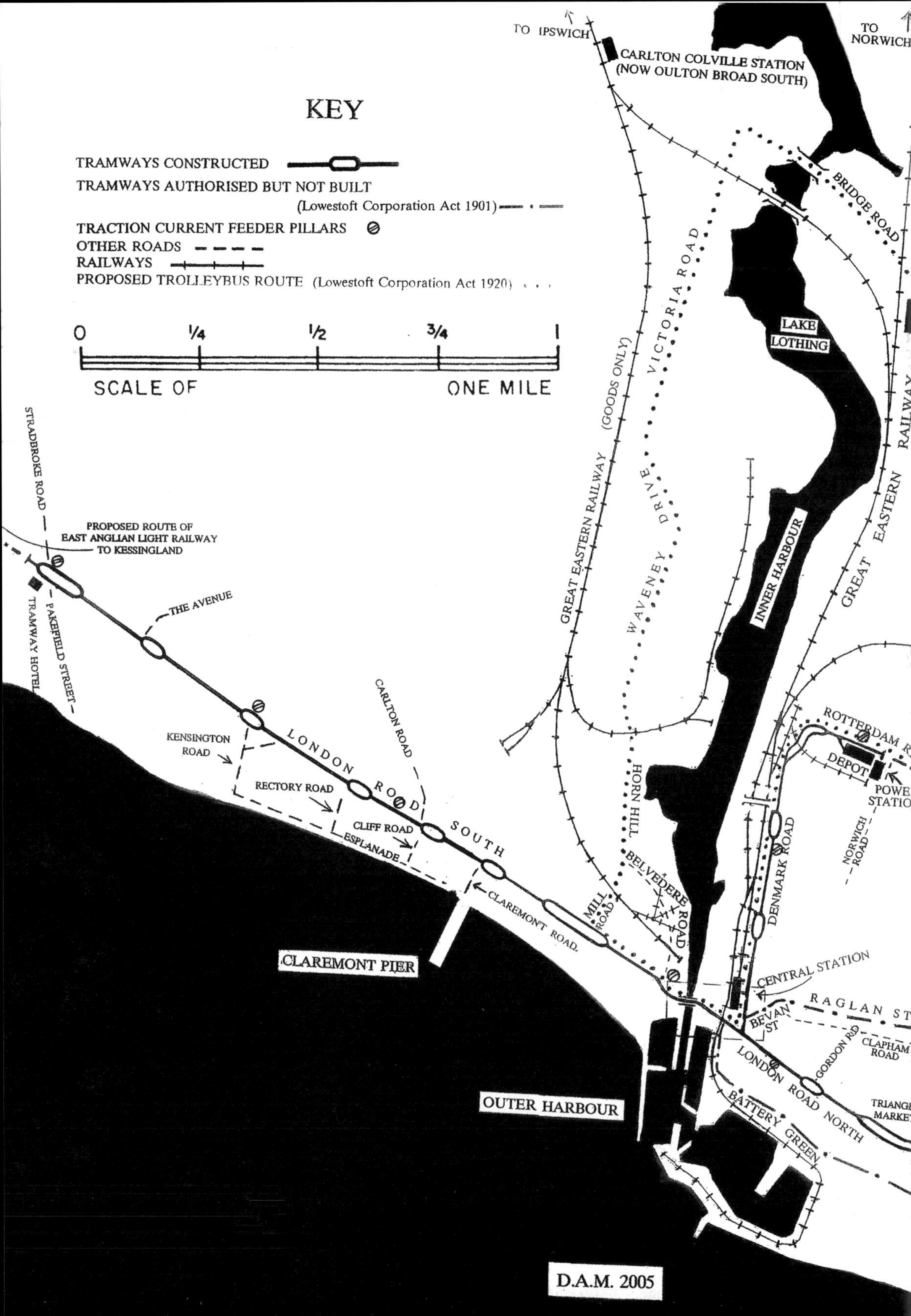

KEY
TRAMWAYS CONSTRUCTED
TRAMWAYS AUTHORISED BUT NOT BUILT
(Lowestoft Corporation Act 1901)
TRACTION CURRENT FEEDER PILLARS
OTHER ROADS
RAILWAYS
PROPOSED TROLLEYBUS ROUTE (Lowestoft Corporation Act 1920)
0
1/4
1/2
3/4
1
SCALE OF ONE MILE
TO IPSWICH
CARLTON COLVILLE STATION
(NOW OULTON BROAD SOUTH)
TO NORWICH
BRIDGE ROAD
VICTORIA ROAD
LAKE LOTHING
GREAT EASTERN RAILWAY (GOODS ONLY)
WAVENEY DRIVE
INNER HARBOUR
GREAT EASTERN RAILWAY
STRADBROKE ROAD
PROPOSED ROUTE OF EAST ANGLIAN LIGHT RAILWAY TO KESSINGLAND
TRAMWAY HOTEL
PAKEFIELD STREET
THE AVENUE
CARLTON ROAD
KENSINGTON ROAD
LONDON ROAD SOUTH
RECTORY ROAD
CLIFF ROAD
ESPLANADE
CLAREMONT ROAD
MILL ROAD
HORN HILL
BELVEDERE ROAD
ROTTERDAM R
DEPOT
POWER STATION
DENMARK ROAD
NORWICH ROAD
CENTRAL STATION
RAGLAN ST
BEVAN ST
GORDON RD
CLAPHAM ROAD
LONDON ROAD NORTH
BATTERY GREEN
TRIANGLE MARKET
CLAREMONT PIER
OUTER HARBOUR
D.A.M. 2005

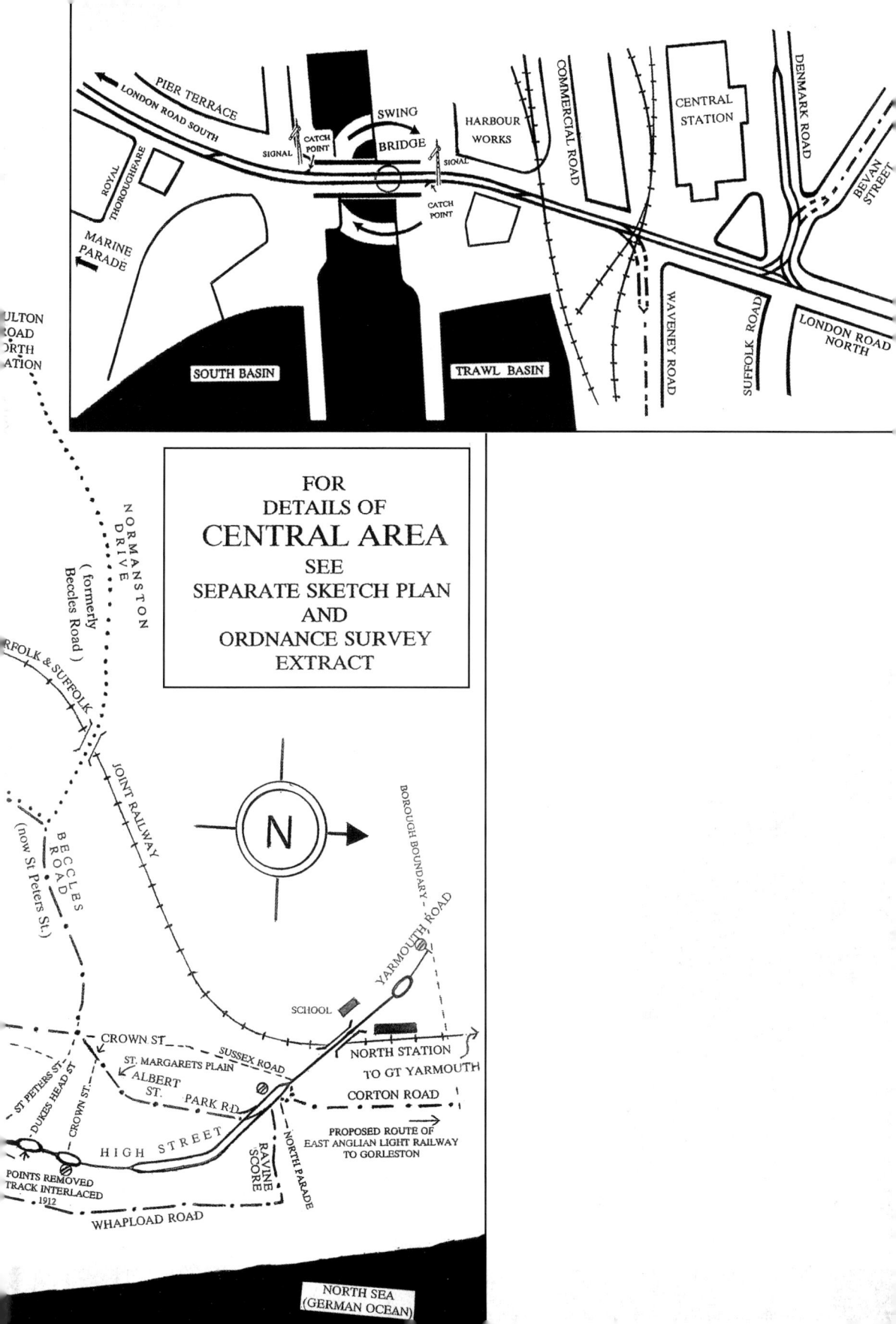

FOR
DETAILS OF
CENTRAL AREA
SEE
SEPARATE SKETCH PLAN
AND
ORDNANCE SURVEY
EXTRACT

GEOGRAPHICAL SETTING

Lowestoft is the furthest north of Suffolk's larger towns and is the most easterly settlement in Britain. It lies on the northern and southern shores of Lake Lothing; believed to have been the former estuary of the river Waveney, which became blocked by a shingle bar. The river now veers broadly north to Breydon Water, about 9 miles (14km) distant, where it joins the river Yare. This, in turn, discharges into the North Sea at Gorleston; 7 miles (11km) to the north of Lowestoft. To the west, Lake Lothing is connected by navigable channel to Oulton Broad; an ancient artificial lake. This is fed by a dyke connecting with the old river. The combined waters now reach the sea via a man made channel in Lowestoft harbour which bisects the modern town. To the north, the old town of Lowestoft looks down from what had been cliff tops to the Denes flat sandy terrain, left by a receding sea. To the south, the land climbs gently through Kirkley and then descends a little to Pakefield. Here, the sea has shown no wish to recede and, until the sea defence measures of the 1930s, had been claiming more and more of this cliff top community. To the west, the town continues to spread itself across the gently undulating plain of the Waveney Valley.

Topography presented no major problems for the tramway builders. The greatest and man made challenge was the swing bridge across the harbour channel.

HISTORICAL BACKGROUND

Lowestoft is mentioned in the Domesday Book (1086) as a small agricultural settlement. It was located on a site in the north of the present town and expanded as a medieval fishing community on the cliff tops along the line of the present High Street where most of the town's oldest buildings remain. Cuts in the cliffs known as 'Scores' became thoroughfares down to The Denes where a quite distinct Beach Village grew up in the 18th and 19th centuries. Major expansion occurred with the arrival of the railway (1847) and development of the harbour. This effectively moved the town centre down the hill from the old High Street to the railway station and harbour area. Lowestoft was eventually to rank as third port nationally in terms of quantities of fish landed. The population more than quadrupled in the second half of the nineteenth century.

A prime mover in the town's economic development was the engineer, entrepreneur and philanthropist Samuel Morton Peto, the "Father of Modern Lowestoft", who also expanded its established role as a fashionable resort by facilitating the building of grand terraces and hotels on what had been deemed worthless land in the then quite separate parish of Kirkley to the south of the harbour. Much of this development survives, though many fine buildings have been lost. Further Victorian development resulted in a continuous built up area for 1 ½ miles (2.4km) southward to Pakefield.

Industries that became associated with Lowestoft mostly related to fishing, shipping and shipbuilding. For about 50 years up to the beginning of the nineteenth century, porcelain was produced. This ware is quite famous and sought after today by collectors. Among industries to arrive later were food processing, general and electrical engineering and coach-building. The latter did not extend to tramcars, however. Over the centuries, there has been continuing rivalry between Lowestoft and its more extrovert neighbour Great Yarmouth 8 miles (12km) to the north. However, modern economic realities have engendered a greater sense of interdependence in recent years as fishing and manufacturing industries have declined in both towns, although the North Sea gas and oil industries are still active. Tourism and the service sector seek to fill the gaps.

The East Anglian Tramway, proposed in 1871, would have passed through Lowestoft on its 20mile (32km) route from Southtown Station, Great Yarmouth to Southwold. Only that part of the route from Southtown to Gorleston was actually opened (1875) but the operator proposed, in 1882, to build a separate horse tram line on the Lowestoft section.. This did not materialise. Neither did an ambitious scheme, in 1898, for a continuous electrically powered East Anglian Light Railway from Caister- 2 miles (3km) north of Great Yarmouth to the coastal village of Kessingland, just over 5miles (8km) south of Lowestoft. Construction of the route north of Lowestoft harbour was succesfully opposed by the railway companies who went on to open a line between Lowestoft and Great Yarmouth in 1903. In 1904 Lowestoft Corporation took over the powers to construct the southern part to Kessingland, subsequently applied to renew them, but never exercised them. Meanwhile they obtained an Act in 1901 enabling them to construct a tramway within the Borough which they then determined to operate themselves.

A considerable amount of street widening had first to be undertaken, which had particular impact at the northern end of the High Street. The inaugural track laying ceremony took place at Pakefield on 11th March 1903. After a herculean effort by the contractors, the 3ft 6ins (1067mm) gauge line north to Belle Vue Park, with a branch in Denmark Road, was opened to traffic just four months later on 22nd July. The 1901 Act also authorised three further lines to Yarmouth Road via Raglan Street, Beccles Road (the modern Peters Street) and the Beach Village or 'The Beach' as it was known locally. These were never built although junctions to provide for them were included in the original track installation. Further track work to the Borough boundary in Yarmouth Road was inspected and given Board of Trade approval in January 1904. This was quite separate from the proposed end-on junction with the (never built) East Anglian Tramway entering the town via Corton Road. The maximum extent of the tramway was just over 4 miles (6.4 km) of which most was single track with passing loops..

The Corporation's application for a parliamentary bill to construct the tramways had met some stiff opposition; notably from certain local business interests who were concerned that the town was saddling itself with a very heavy financial commitment. This resistance softened, when the Corporation decided to confine itself to building a trunk line. It would have been awakened had they decided to proceed with the branches allowed for in the 1901 Act and with the construction of the light railway to Kessingland. Even the cost of the basic system went beyond the Board of Trade sanctional limit. The Corporation's approach to further expenditure on developing the tramways was, consequently, cautious. There was some retrenchment and recourse to economies from the earliest years. A scheduled service along Denmark Road was an early casualty although passengers were allowed to use cars making their long and usually unremunerative journeys to and from the depot. Extending the double track which would have improved the service and significantly reduced the wear and tear on both installation and rolling stock was briefly considered but ruled out. Heavy expenditure on rectifying the original and, as it transpired, defective track structure in 1910 and 1912 was unavoidable. The view of Mr Bruce, the manager, was that development could generate a return on the capital invested in the Denmark Road line and, in 1908 he proposed a light railway from Rotterdam Road to Oulton Broad; presumably along what is now Normanston Drive. He also suggested a "trackless trolley" (trolleybus) line to Kessingland as a cheaper option than a light railway. Both routes would have passed outside the then Borough boundaries and the Corporation evidently did not find Mr Bruce's economic arguments sufficiently compelling. In 1912 United Automobile Services was established in the town at a time when the Great Eastern railway was withdrawing from omnibus operations. In additon to operating bus routes in the wider locality, the company carved out territory for itself in areas shortly to be incorporated into the Borough and where the Corporation might subsequently have hoped to expand its own services including into Oulton Broad. The Corporation had 'missed the boat' and never established themselves as the dominant transport operator in the enlarged Lowestoft. Although for a period in the 1970's joint working with the Eastern Counties Omnibus Company enabled Council owned buses to range in the western extremities of the town, the writing had been on the wall for the maroon and primrose fleet, which succumbed when Waveney District Council finally resolved to sell in 1977.

During World War I, Lowestoft became a front line town and its existing role as a naval base was expanded. In 1916, it was shelled by German warships and bombed by Zeppelins. The depot and 2 cars suffered damage. 60 staff were called to military service of whom 11 did not return. Women were recruited and kept the service going. The tramway was in a very run down condition when hostilities ceased.

The track, in particular, was coming to the end of its economic life; extensive welding repairs and replacements using second hand rail being undertaken between 1922 and 1925.

The 1920 Lowestoft Corporation Act contained permissive powers for the construction of a circular trolleybus line from the town centre to Oulton Broad (as shown on the map). However, the Act stipulated that this could only proceed if the Ministry of Transport could first be persuaded that the existing bus service, provided by United, was inadequate or inefficient. This would possibly have entailed a costly and, probably, fruitless legal process and no trolleybus line was built. In 1924, the Lighting Sub-Committee approved the use of surplus traction columns and span wires to suspend street lights in parts of Rotterdam Road and Normanston Drive. Coincidentally, this was on the line of the proposed trolleybus route but the poles were planted vertically and not raked to take the weight of overhead work. The Corporation technically kept its options open in respect of trolleybuses but ultimately decided on motorbuses to replace the trams. The author has found nothing in municipal or Ministry records to substantiate anecdotal accounts of trolleybus trials in the town.

Powers to operate buses were obtained and, in 1927, the first two Guy single deckers were purchased to augment the trams. These operated on a sight-seeing service along the northern sea wall and on a short lived unsuccessful route at the 'back of the town'. With the arrival of more vehicles in 1928, bus journeys; extended to the north Borough boundary, were also inserted in the tram schedules. Two years later the decision was made to replace the trams with motor buses and with the aim of removing the tracks by 1935. This was brought forward to 1931 when the Corporation was able to offset the labour costs with government aid for the relief of unemployment.

The last tram (car 2), driven by Noah Rudd and decorated with a wreath of arum lilies, ran on the night of 8th May 1931. It was given a rousing send off. A piece of 'verse' attached to the car was attributed (without certainty) to the then Manager Mr. Herbert Saunders.

" This is the last of the poor old trams.
They've done their bit when the shed door slams.
For years they've rolled you black and blue.
Now, they'll get peace and so will you."

LOWESTOFT CORPORATION TRAMWAYS.

The Mayor and Corporation Request the pleasure of the Company of

Mr. ...Councillor Chapman... and Lady

At the Inaugural Ceremony of the Running of the Electrical Tramways, Wednesday, July 22nd, 1903.

MEET AT CAR DEPOT, ROTTERDAM ROAD, 11.30.

THE MAYOR WILL DRIVE THE FIRST CAR AT 12.15.

ROTTERDAM ROAD

1. On the opening day, 22nd July 1903, the Mayor, Mr Lancelot Orde, stands at the controls of the leading car of a procession of four trams. To his right is the Town Clerk, Mr P. Beattie Nicholson. The location is Rotterdam Road, just outside the depot. The house in the background stands in Laundry Lane which was later renamed Eastern Way after Eastern Coach Works had been established there. (Author's coll)

2. Of the last two cars in the opening procession, this single decker conveyed engineers and contractors, while the double decker behind carried representatives of the local and technical press. The driver of the tram adopts a haughty pose, while the chap in charge of the adjacent landau looks disinclined to stage a race. (P.Jenkins coll)

DENMARK ROAD

3. Our journey with the opening procession now takes us around the corner from Rotterdam Road into Denmark Road. The Mayor has an inspector at his elbow, while other civic dignitaries lurk in the shrubbery behind. Close to this point, a railway siding was constructed from the Corporation sidings near Coke Ovens Junction (left) to the Corporation power station (right); crossing the tram tracks on the level. (P.Jenkins coll)

4. Pictures showing trams in Denmark Road have proved hard to find. This view shows the eastern end by the railway station in 1929. By this time, buildings in front of the station had been cleared to create an open plain.. (Compare the scene in picture 35.) The picture is also significant in that the photographer appears to have used panchromatic film which has portrayed the rather striking tramcar livery much more brightly than in most other photographs of the period. (C.Wilson / Mrs. J. Plant coll)

LONDON ROAD NORTH

5. We now commence our journey along London Road North. The tracks from Denmark Road emerge from the left. The date is before 1913 as Leach's ironmongery shop on the corner of Suffolk Road (right) suffered a conflagration in that year. The site is today occupied by HSBC bank. The whole of London Road North is now a pedestrian precinct. (B.Gowen coll)

PYKE, JEWELLER
LEIGHTON'S
DINNERS
TEAS
SUPPERS
DENTAL SURGERY
G.S.NUNN

← 6. The same stretch of street is depicted here as seen looking south from near the corner of Beach Road. The clearance between the tram and a motor car inconsiderately parked adjacent to the stop and passing loop appears to be very tight. This piece of street is readily identifiable today and three of the upper storey bay windows survive. (P. Killby coll)

← 7. A few strides further on, this northward view of London Road displays a sylvan aspect which it has since totally lost. Shops now stand where the trees and gardens once graced the scene. To the left, part of the late Victorian House behind survives today as the Pantry Cafe and facing onto Surrey St (off left). The bay windows to the right are of Chadds store which still trades today although now owned by Palmers of Great Yarmouth. This is an early tramway view as the 1903 built car has yet to have advertising applied. (A. D. Packer coll)

8. A little further north two motor cars on wedding duty outside the Baptist Church attract admiring glances from outside the Army & Navy stores, while a tram has stopped by the Marina Corner further up the road. In this pre 1914 period, there would always be a tram in view in London Road North. (A.D. Packer coll)

HOT & COLD
BATH
OVERY'S
HAIRDRESSING
SALOONS
DYERS
REFRESHMENTS

EASTAUGH & SON

← 9. From much the same vantage point, two trams can be seen just to have passed each other. No wedding cars wait by the Baptist Church and its grounds. These have since given way to the modern edifice of Boots store. Many of the small house to shop conversions on the left survive today with modern frontages. (Studio 161)

← 10. Looking south, in about 1910, we see northbound car 6 passing the stop by the corner of Marina Road (left). Wheatley's airy looking Home Furnishings store has since gone and the single storey Savers Toiletries and Health Care now occupies the site. The Marina Theatre, sign posted on the corner of Wheatley's is, thankfully, still with us. (P. Killby coll)

11. Facing north, in the late 1920's, we find Woolworths on the west side of the road. It continued to trade from a more modern building until closed in 2009. QD stores have stepped into the breach. Car 15 is heading north, preceded by a single deck bus of United Automobile Services, which was founded in Lowestoft in 1912.
(P. Rasbery coll)

12. On the eastern side of the road, the crowd besieging LeGrice's store suggests that the advertising carried on car 11 has had an instantaneous and dramatic effect! Just beyond is the entrance to the United Methodist Church on the site of a present day sports wear shop. The spire of this church can be seen in picture 8. The auctioneers' buildings on the further corner of Gordon Road survive in altered form as Clarks shoe store. (C. Wilson / Mrs. J. Plant / P. Killby coll)

13. Transferring our gaze north westwards enables us to take in the whole of the Gordon Road crossing, as it appeared about 1904. What appears to be a Chapel to the right is the purpose built YMCA building of 1886; closed in 1965. Two of the gables (left) survive today amidst the bland functional architecture which has overtaken so much of London Road North following the bombing in World War II and general redevelopement since. (Studio 161)

14. In Edwardian days, two ladies are given gentlemanly assistance while boarding car 7. To the left, the sale of "motors, cycles and accessories" is obviously sound business. To the right, two young men survey the scene and the photographer from the premises of O Rogers. Rogers published a range of local postcards of which this was one. (P. Rasbery coll)

15. A little further north, our tour coincides with the opening day procession as it approaches the crest of the gentle hill of London Road North and enters the last passing loop before the thoroughfare becomes the High Street. Milton Road (right) faces The Volunteer public house (left) with the more abstemious Congregational Church adjoining and behind the ladies in straw boaters. This church is the only survivor today of the three places of worship, passed by the trams, in London Road North. (Mrs. B. Killett coll)

HIGH STREET

16.   After a short stretch of the High Street, we come to the Triangle Market which is seen here in 1913. In that year, the contract for advertising on the cars was temporarily ended and the upper deck panels were painted plain red. The previous year, interlaced track seen in the foreground replaced points and a loop between 95 and 129 High Street as a cost-saving measure. Today, the Triangle is dominated by the Eastern Sails; a modern awning which also performs as street sculpture. (A. D. Packer coll)

1927 map.

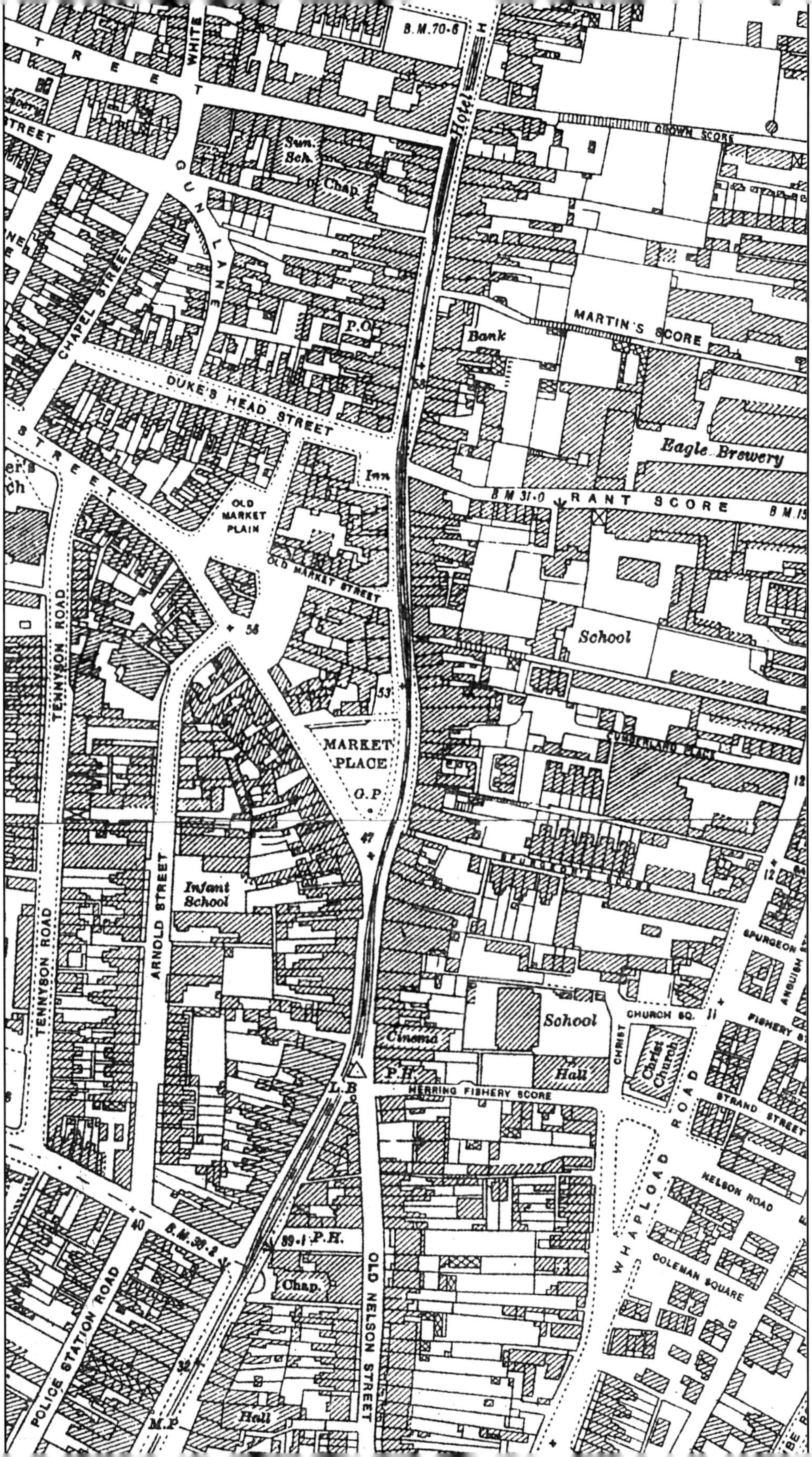
WHITE
STREET
B.M.70·6
Hotel
CROWN SCORE
Sun. Sch.
Chap.
GUN LANE
CHAPEL STREET
P.O.
Bank
MARTIN'S SCORE
DUKE'S HEAD STREET
Eagle Brewery
Inn
B.M 31·0
RANT SCORE
OLD MARKET PLAIN
OLD MARKET STREET
School
56
53
MARKET PLACE
G.P.
TENNYSON ROAD
47
ARNOLD STREET
Infant School
SPURGEON
ANGUISH
CHURCH SQ.
FISHERY
School
Cinema
CHRIST
Christ Church
P.H.
Hall
L.B.
HERRING FISHERY SCORE
STRAND STREET
NELSON ROAD
WHAPLOAD ROAD
COLEMAN SQUARE
40
B.M.30·2
39·1
P.H.
Chap.
OLD NELSON STREET
POLICE STATION ROAD
32
M.P.
Hall

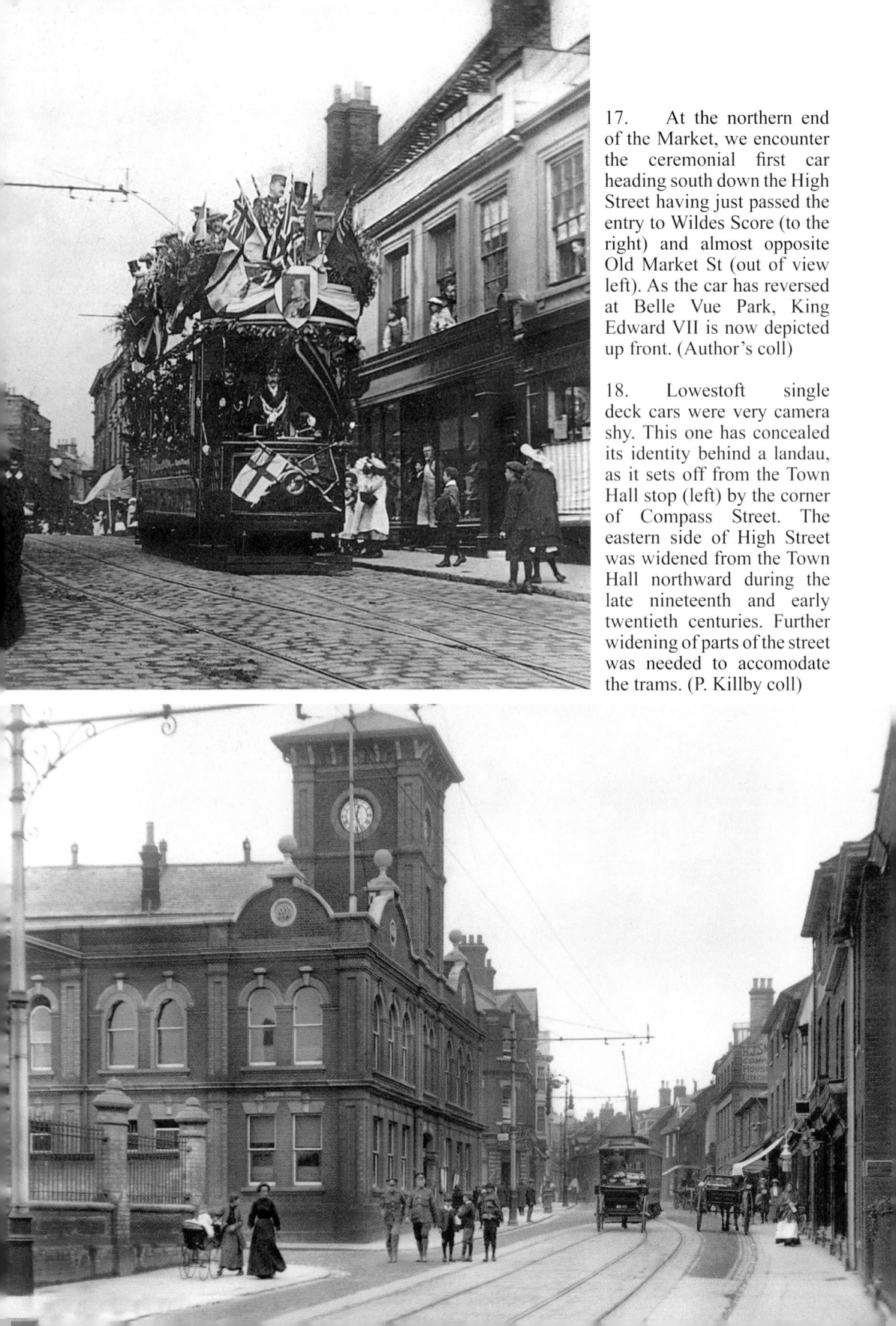

17. At the northern end of the Market, we encounter the ceremonial first car heading south down the High Street having just passed the entry to Wildes Score (to the right) and almost opposite Old Market St (out of view left). As the car has reversed at Belle Vue Park, King Edward VII is now depicted up front. (Author's coll)

18. Lowestoft single deck cars were very camera shy. This one has concealed its identity behind a landau, as it sets off from the Town Hall stop (left) by the corner of Compass Street. The eastern side of High Street was widened from the Town Hall northward during the late nineteenth and early twentieth centuries. Further widening of parts of the street was needed to accomodate the trams. (P. Killby coll)

19. At the very northern end of the High Street, car 1 is on a short working to Central Station; possibly before returning to the depot with conductor Frederick Mitchell and his driver in charge. Car 1 has received battle honours in the form of a dent to its dash plate. The wall to the left fronted a convalescent home. The modern North Lowestoft Methodist Church now occupies part of this site.
(P. Mitchell coll)

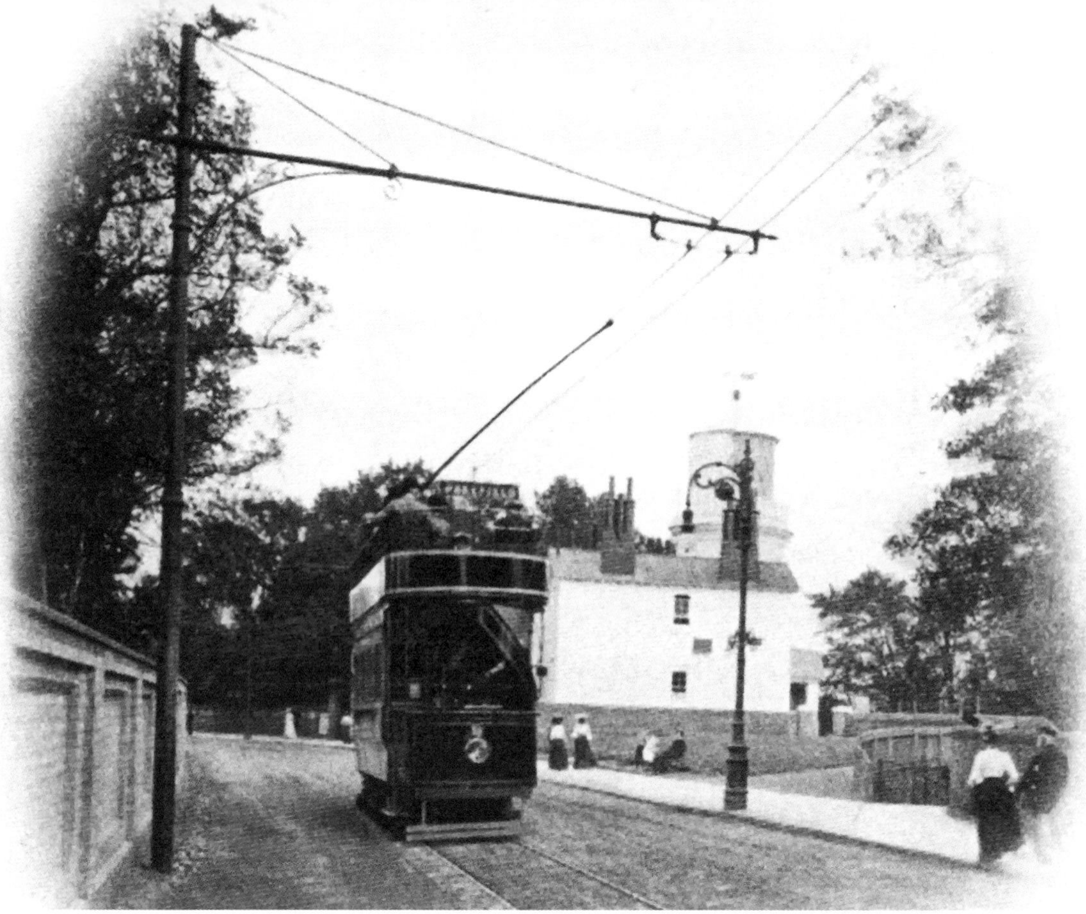

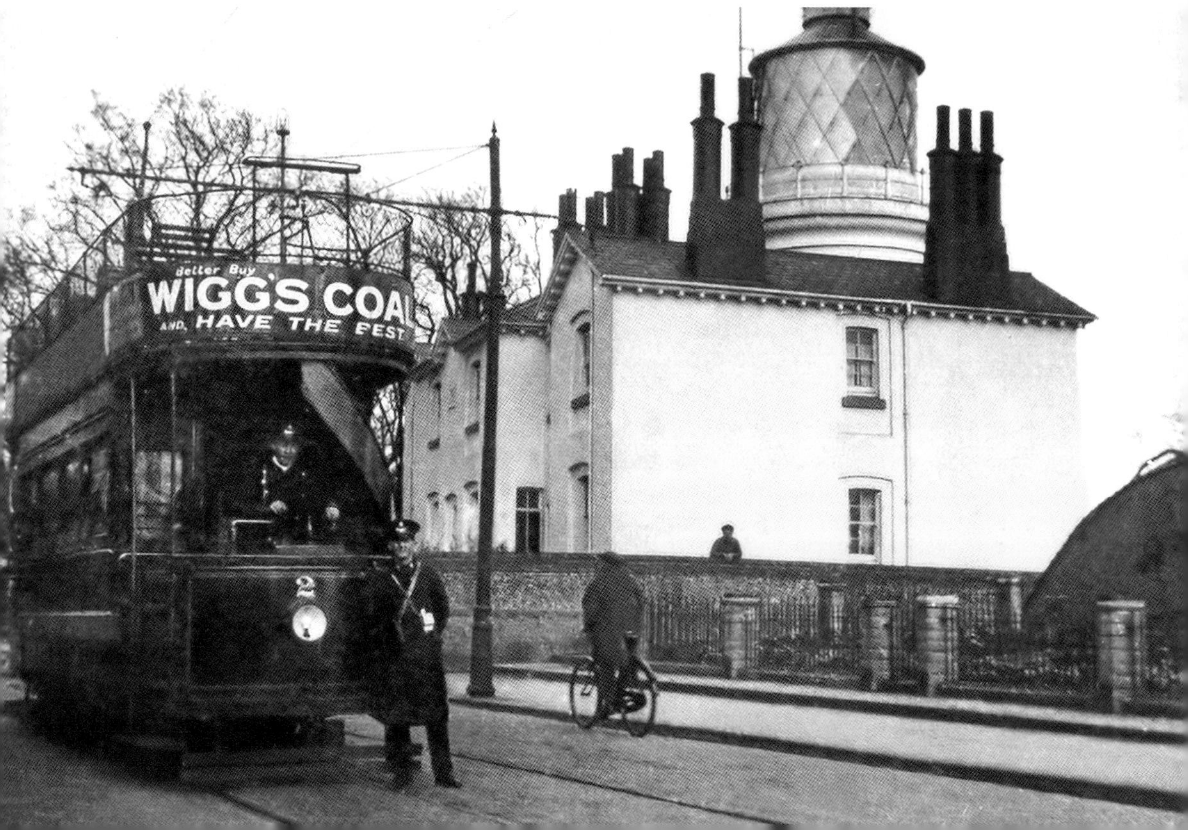
Better Buy
WIGG'S COAL
AND, HAVE THE BEST

← 20. The road is still technically the High Street as it opens out on the cliff top in the vicinity of the High Light. (There was a Low Light on the beach for many years). The High Light dates from 1874 and went over to fully automatic operation just over a century later. It occupies the site of an earlier High Light constructed in 1676, while Samuel Pepys was Master Of Trinity House. (R J Harley coll))

← 21. Towards the end of the tramway era, Car 2 and crew are snapped by the High Light. The tram appears to be running wrong line in this double track section so a passing cyclist decides to do the same. To the right is the First World War tank which, between the two world wars, stood as a monument in the small ornamental garden. (J. Herd coll)

22. This scene by the High Light dates from 1904 when car 14 was brand new. Behind is the entrance to the Sparrow's Nest, a public park. A theatre of the same name was built here in 1913 and was a popular entertainment venue until demolition in 1991. The elaborate original painting of traction columns and street lighting is well portrayed. (Studio 161)

YARMOUTH ROAD

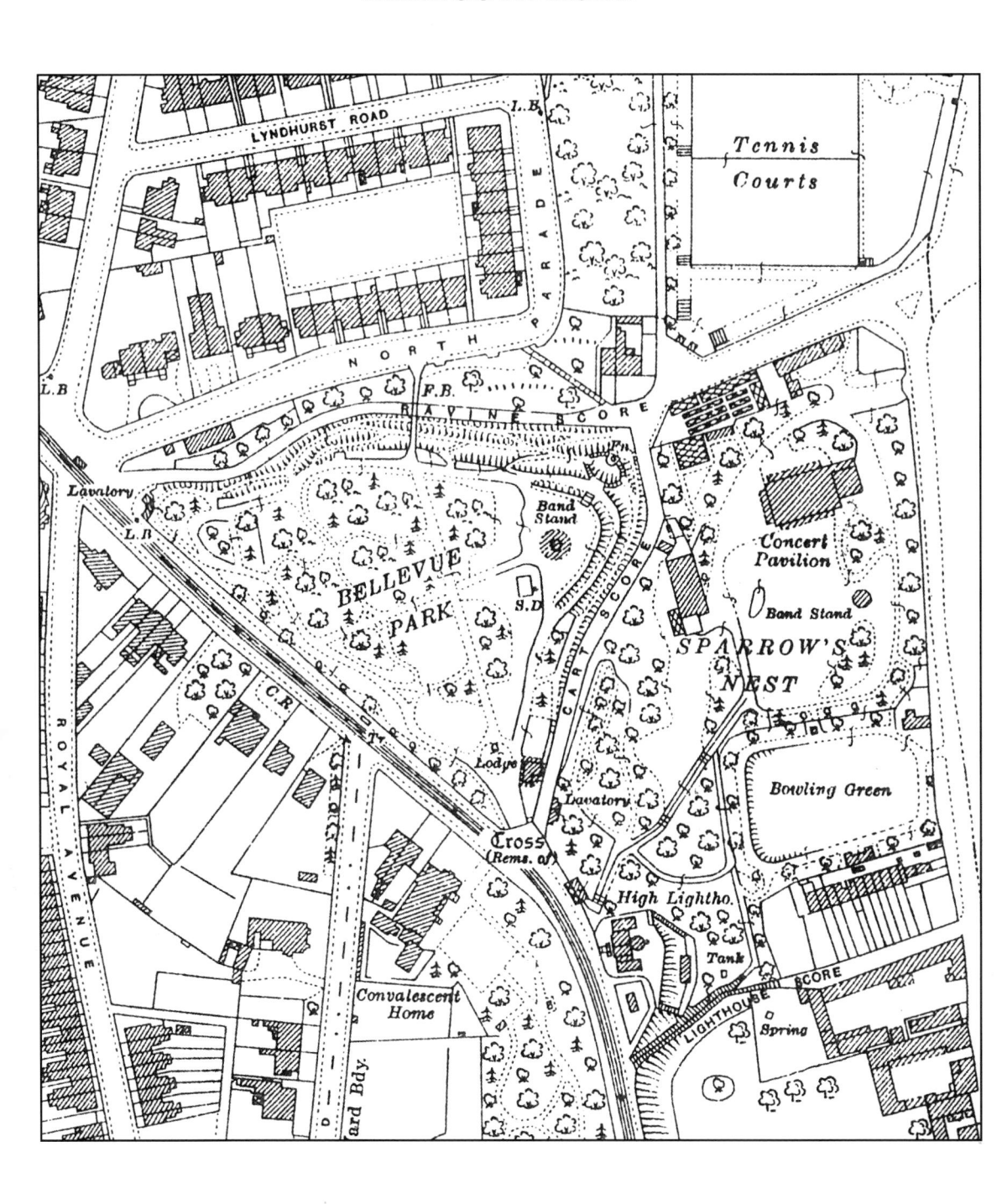

23. Having passed around the bend depicted in picture 22 we look back towards the High Light and to the Sparrow's Nest entrance. The crossover here being installed became useful for short workings to coincide with the end of the shows at Sparrow's Nest theatre when as many as 12 cars were needed to convey members of the audience away.
(Author's coll)

24. The crew of car 6 seem determined on their work as they wait at the 1903 temporary northern terminus by Belle Vue park. The remainder of the line northwards to the Borough boundary was approved by the Board of Trade in January 1904.
(National Tramway Museum coll)

25. At the same location, but a quarter of a century later, two cars are drawn up to depict the closing days of the tramway era. The conductor of car 14 is Charles Boon. The railings seen here have since been removed so Belle Vue Park now enjoys a more open aspect. (East Anglia Transport Museum coll)

26. A single deck car heading south approaches the Belle Vue stop about 1905. The kink in the track appears to coincide with the pointwork for the projected Junction into Park Road (left). The man clearing the road is doing a service to the community in general and to rhubarb growers in particular. (East Anglia Transport Museum coll)

27. Points were laid in 1903 at the junction of Yarmouth Road and Park Road for the authorised line via Raglan Street which was never built. These were removed in 1909. A similar set of points at the proposed junction with Ravine Score were taken out at the same time.
(Reproduced from the Lowestoft Borough Archives, courtesy of Waveney District Council)

28. For most of the life of the tramway the regular northern terminus was at North Parade. Here, in 1922, conductor Henry Friston and his driver are about to transport a contingent of boy scouts, who have piled kit onto the driver's platform. A card fixed to the dash suggests that the car has been hired especially. The passenger shelter, built around a traction column, is nudging up against a shed telephone box of the National Telephone Company.
(D. Friston coll)

29.   Car 15 of the 1904 batch is here seen at North Parade terminus, looking south east, in the late 1920s. The day is obviously a warm one as two of the drop light windows are lowered to reveal a couple of cloche hats worn by passengers in the saloon. The white colouring of the fender is a theatre bill for the Sparrow's Nest show (see picture 106) (Photographer unknown/ Author's coll)

➜ 30.   Car 13 (also from the 1904 batch) is stopped on Yarmouth Road and just north of the junction with Sussex Road. The next stop is North Station.. In 1910, regular services were cut back to the previous stop at North Parade.(J. Herd coll)

➜ 31.   This is the most northerly location depicted in this book. Bogie car 24 is having its trolley turned on the bridge adjacent to Lowestoft North Station from whence it will proceed to Central Station. The destination display, being imprecise, is correct for both directions of travel! The fine little North Station was opened on 13th July 1903 and just days before the Corporation tramways. It closed in 1970. Today, housing occupies the site. A slight hump in the road betrays the former location of the bridge. (National Tramway Museum coll)

JOHN DEVEREU
GROCERS & PROVISION
127-8-9 HIGH St ALSO
C.R. PYKE
46 LONDON Rd N. OPPOSITE POST OFFICE
FOR PRESENTS AND SOUVENIRS
WEDDING RINGS
LOWESTOFT CORPORATION TRAMWAYS

RAILWAY STATION
24

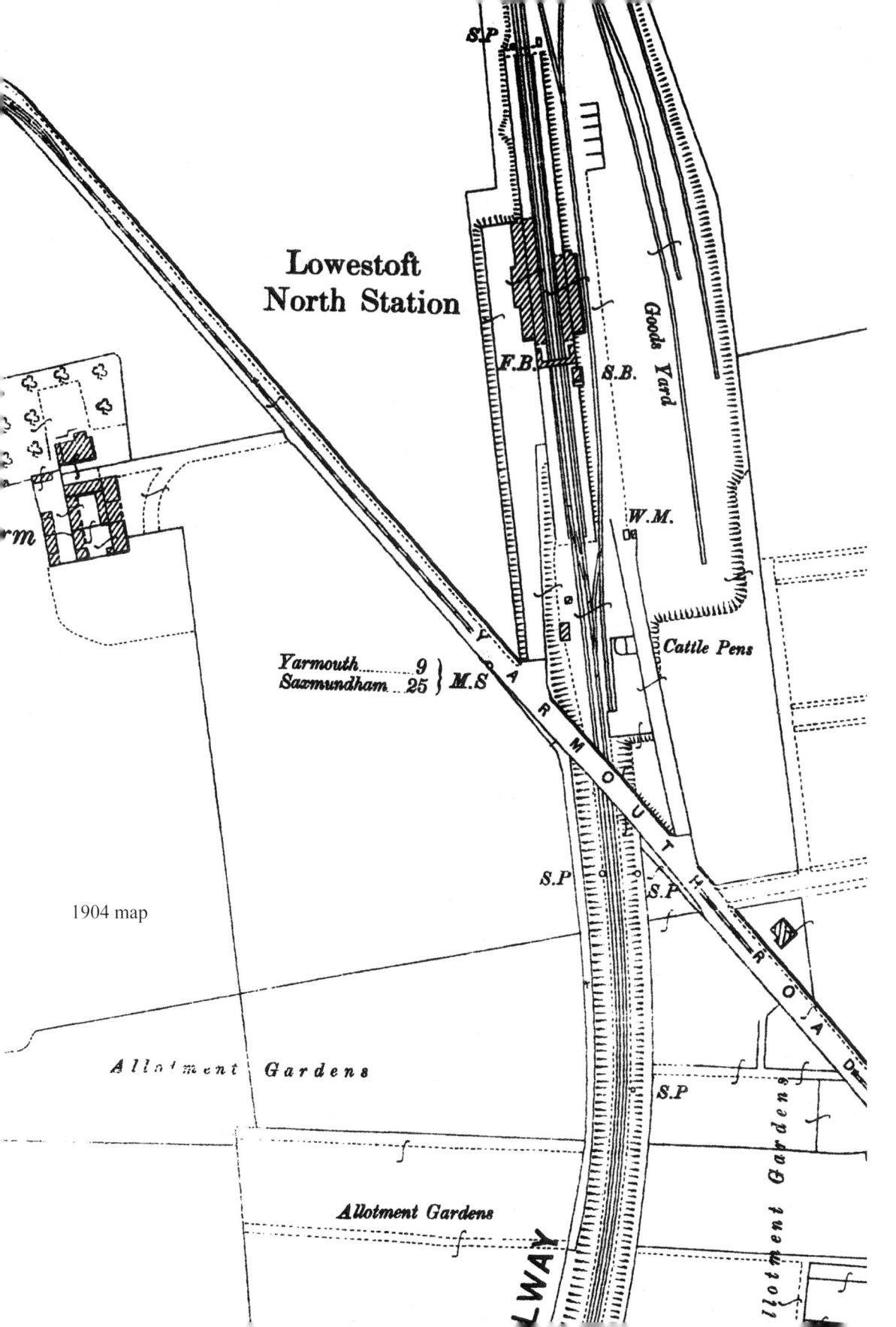

Lowestoft
North Station

F.B. S.B.

Goods Yard

W.M.

Cattle Pens

Yarmouth .... 9 } M.S
Saxmundham ... 25

S.P

1904 map

Allotment Gardens

S.P

Allotment Gardens

32. Car 4 is also depicted at the North Station although the destination blind only extends to Belle Vue Park. The track from here for the remaining 500 or so yards, to the North Borough boundary was used very little including for specials and a short-lived Sunday afternoon country air service in the tramway's early days. Lifting the track for reuse elsewhere was considered as early as 1909 and records suggest that it was raided for materials in 1915. Formal Board of Trade approval for its removal was granted in 1918.
(Southerden Collection, Newham Archives & Local Studies Library)

STATION SQUARE

33.　　We retrace our steps southward for a mile to the corner of Denmark Road (right) and London Road North. We last "stood" here with picture 5 looking north. Car 13 has encountered unlucky conditions; almost certainly as a consequence of an exceptionally high tide in 1905. The crew have neglected to rewind the destination indicator and are heading north and not south to Pakefield, where they would probably have preferred to remain. (P. Killby coll)

34. Across the road from the previous vantage point we rejoin the opening procession now heading south. The Mayor has temporarily relinquished control of the car to the inspector. Since picture 17, King Edward VII has taken refuge behind our national flag. (East Anglia Transport Museum coll)

35. The street scene at the previous location is more fully depicted in this perspective from the corner of Waveney Road. The Bon Marche store by which the processional tram was standing is pin pointed by the awning to the right. The buildings (including the station master's house) which stood in front of the station are seen to the left. Compare with the same location as seen in picture 4. The junction with Denmark Road is just behind the trees making a cramped site for a triangular tramway track installation. The traction column carries one of the long 18ft (5.4m) brackets stretching over two tracks. The bank (right) is on the corner of Waveney Road. (A. Brotchie coll)

1904 map

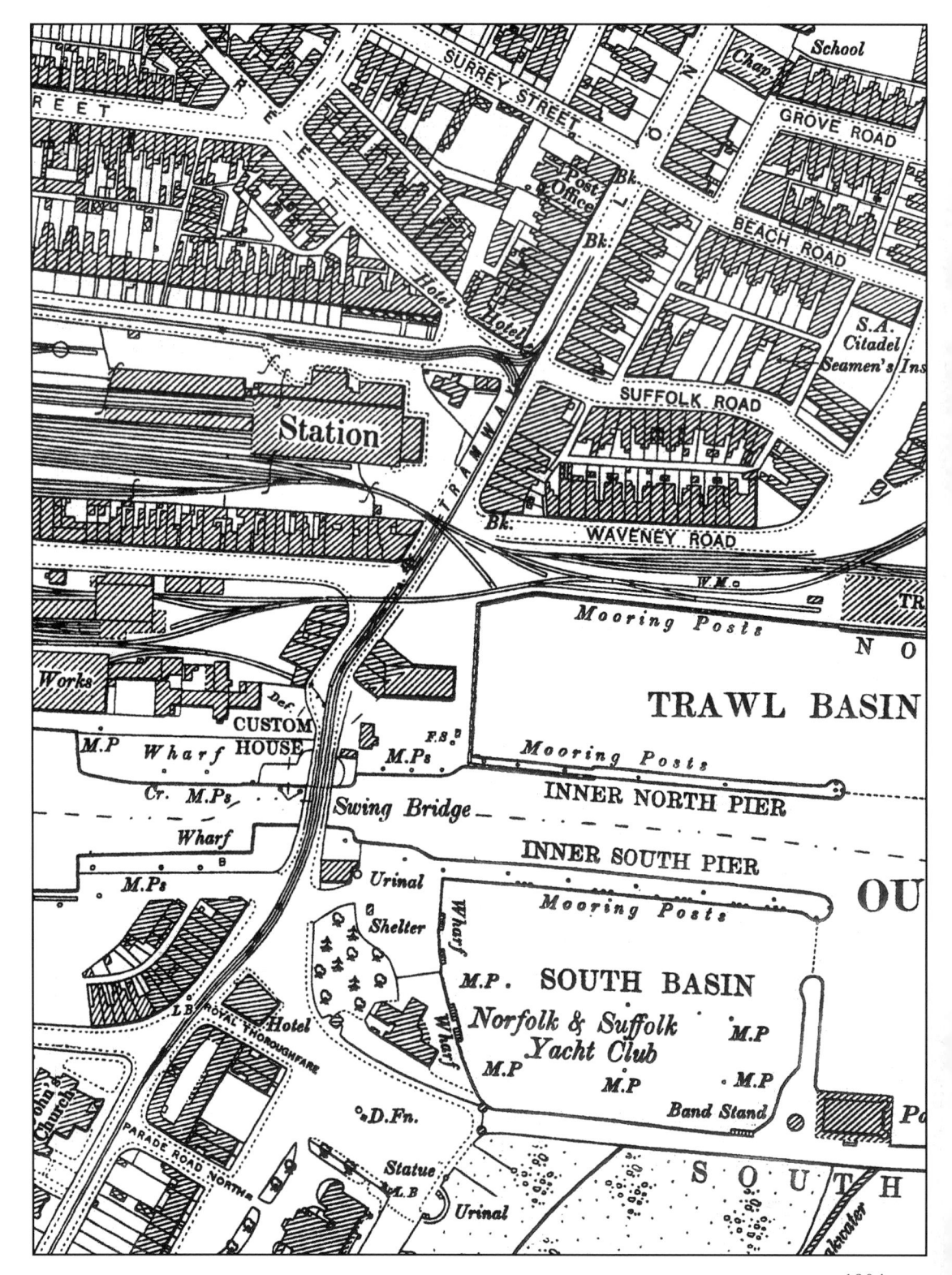

36.   Just south of Waveney Road, the tramway was crossed by railway tracks running from the station yard to the harbour and fish dock. A 1904 car has here collided with a railway van which has escaped the station confines.. The tram has ended up turned through a right angle and abreast of its adversary. Shunting horses can just be glimpsed at the far end of the van. Records suggest that this encounter occurred in 1912. The rail crossing was last used in 1973 and is now lifted.
(P. Kilby coll)

37.   From just beyond the rail crossing, we glance back to the north from whence we have just come. The bank on the corner of Waveney Road is now a cafe. (A. D. Packer coll)

38. Turning in the opposite direction (south), we get our first glimpse of the environs of the bridge which is open for the passage of the sailing trawler LT67 Willing Boys. Two trams have to join the queue of waiting traffic. In the foreground are the tracks of another rail crossing to the harbour; in this case from the Great Eastern Railway Harbour Works. The scene dates from about 1913. (Studio 161)

39.　The ornamental entrance to what had become the London & North Eastern Rly Harbour Works is here seen to the left. The buildings (right) are in Commercial Road. The workmen are using a pneumatic drill to loosen up the setts preparatory to the removal of the tram tracks in 1931. The rail/tramway crossing is on the extreme left. A supermarket now occupies the former works site. (C.Wilson coll)

40.　One of the 1903 double deckers here passes over the rail crossing by Commercial Road shortly after World War I. The waist and rocker panels of Lowestoft cars were of steel rather than the more usual mahogany. Dents sustained during wartime conditions have been simply painted over. (J.Herd coll)

41.   After a few strides and looking north, we again see the excavation work portrayed in picture 39. Removal of the track is the priority. The overhead can wait until later. The bus is not a tram replacement but a Leyland Titan TD1 of United Automobile services and running on the route to Oulton Broad, which the Corporation might have served with trolleybuses. It was shortly to be repainted in the livery of the new Eastern Counties Omnibus Company into which United's Norfolk and Suffolk operations were absorbed with effect from July 1931. (C.Wilson coll)

42. Just a few yards on, but a generation earlier, architecture and street furniture are found to be much the same but trams including number 4 dominate the traffic. The path of the rail crossing into the harbour precincts behind the railings to the right can be discerned. (P. Rasbery coll)

43. Seen from the point on the pavement where the boys in the previous picture were standing, a brand new car 5 seems to have been stolen by one of their school friends! In fact, the driver is probably a man of small stature awaiting issue of a non-standard size uniform. There is a curious juxtaposition of poles at the left of the picture. (Author's coll)

44. About twenty five yards and as many years further on, car 9 has just run off the bridge on 21st April 1929. The posture of the tram's suspension gives the illusion that it is towing what appears to be a Ford Model T pick up truck that is perilously close behind. The tram's speed over the bridge and its approaches was, in fact, limited to 6 mph by Board of Trade regulations.
(Dr H.Nicol /National Tramway Museum)

THE BRIDGE

The first bridge over what was to become the harbour channel was opened in 1830. A replacement hydraulically powered swing bridge was completed in 1897. As with the rest of the harbour works, this was controlled by the Great Eastern Railway. (London & North Eastern Railway after 1923).

The 1903 tramway across the bridge was constructed to give a clear passage for the masts and rigging of sailing craft. The overhead was, therefore, a self-supporting structure, which swung with the bridge. Aluminium was used instead of steel and copper to reduce weight. The mechanical connection with the main overhead was made and broken by a slight tilting movement of the bridge immediately at the beginning of its opening and end of its closure.

Mechanical and electrical connections were interlocked with the bridge operating mechanism. When the bridge was open to navigation, the traction current was automatically turned off for a short distance each side. In addition, interlocking catch points were installed to prevent coasting trams accidentally running into the harbour. Sliding safety barriers shut off the carriageway and footways. The Board of Trade required a visual warning system for tram drivers. Railway type semaphore signals were, therefore, installed by 1905 and the Corporation paid the railway a quarterly charge (initially £10) to operate them. Years after the trams ceased to run and following a series of break downs, the ageing swing bridge failed completely in 1969. A replacement bascule bridge was eventually opened in 1972. It too has had a chequered history in recent years. Although now less frequent than in tramway days, the vital openings of the bridge still cut the town in two and can play havoc with passenger timetables and personal schedules alike.

45. The narrow footways on the bridge were often quite crowded in the summer, particularly just after the reopening to traffic, by which time quite an additional crush would have accumulated each side. The flags and pennants in the yacht basin suggest that this is Regatta Week which will have attracted an additional throng. The pagoda like building to the left is the bridge observation and control cabin against which is a rolling traffic barrier. The tracks for this can be seen in the roadway at right angles to the tram rails. (A. D. Packer coll)

46.   The setting evening sun catches the flank of car 12 as it crosses the bridge in a northerly direction. This poor quality but dramatic image conveys the tight fit of the double track tramway against the bridge girders.. Only one tram was permitted on the bridge at any one time.
(J.Herd coll)

47.   This is a very early view of a car crossing the bridge as this single decker is not yet fitted with advertisement panels. At the northern (left hand) end of the bridge is the pole and flag which signalled the bridge being closed to navigation. In this instance, the playing of the wind on the flag has been frozen by the camera to portray the outline of a maritime disaster on the horizon! The prominent building in the middle background is the metal-framed South Pier Pavillion of 1891 which was demolished in 1954. (G. Smith coll)

48. A similar perspective of the bridge is here seen from the tramway's later days. One car heading north across the bridge is about to encounter another heading south. An arrival on the scene since the previous picture was taken is the cabin resembling a small railway signal box. This is believed to have housed the backup bridge winding gear which could be called upon in the event of failure of the main hydraulic mechanism.(G. Smith coll)

49. The ironwork of the bridge can here be seen in detail as the lead car of the opening procession heads south. The gas lamp on the left and its three companions at the other corners of the bridge were removed as a safety measure shortly after tramway services commenced.
(C. Hood coll)

↑ 50. Views of the bridge looking west are rare. This picture is from about 1904 by which time the gas lamps on the corner pillars had been removed.. Tall masts grace the skyline above the inner harbour as do the sheerlegs used to install steam machinery in locally built vessels. Beyond the bridge can be seen the Custom House, Jacobean style Harbour Master's house and the iron works with its chimneys. (R. Adderson coll)

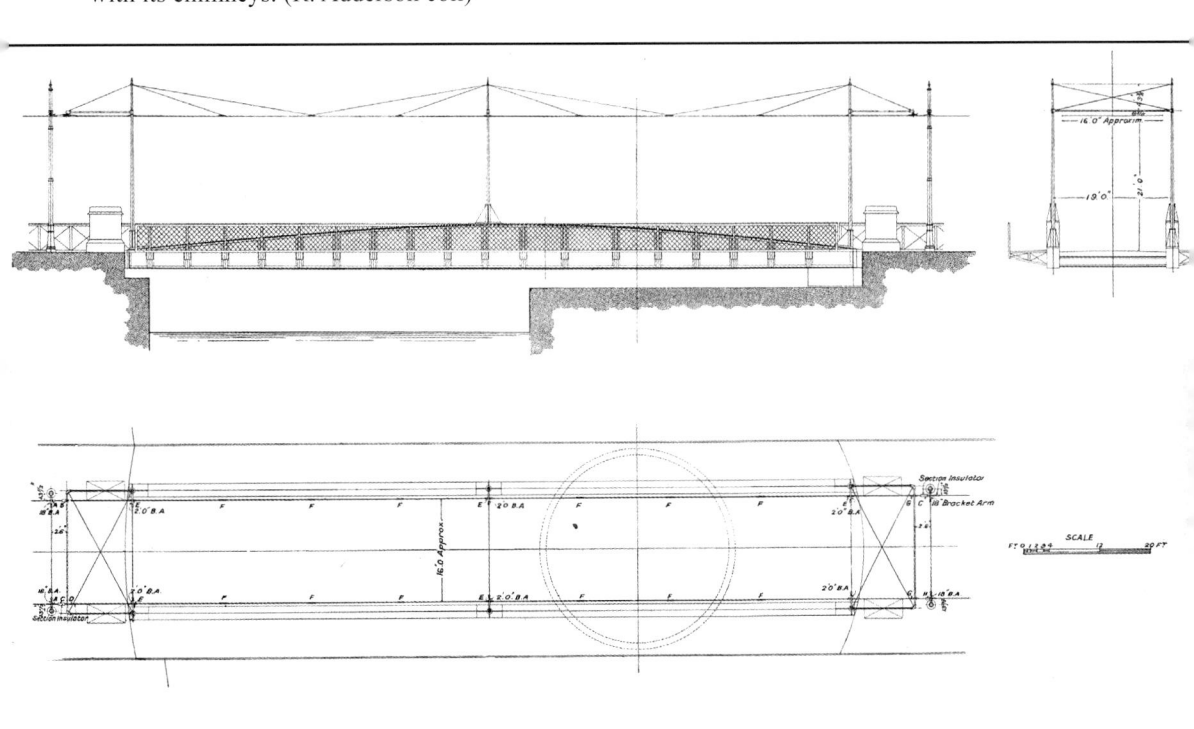

↓ 51. From the bridge, this view of the outer harbour shows the installation of the tramway power connection across the harbour channel. The cable, sheathed in iron pipes, was lowered onto the channel bed from a row of boats moored as pontoons. This scheme was devised by the Borough Engineer (and, later, Tramway Manager) Mr Bruce. The cost of his scheme was a quarter of the lowest tender submitted by an outside contractor.
(Tramway & Railway World / National Tramway Museum)

52. An unidentified car is seen crossing the bridge when the tramway installation was almost brand new. Two flags are hoisted to signal to approaching shipping that the bridge is closed to navigation. The gentle rise of London Road North can be seen receding into the left distance. (Studio 161)

53. Also seen from the southern side, the swing bridge is open for the seaward passage of a stream drifter. A tram and other traffic wait on the northern side; the tram having come as close to the bridge as the safety arrangements permitted. (National Tramway Museum coll)

54. This is a very early view of car 7 passing southwards over the bridge. The traction columns and bridge overhead have not yet been painted in their top coats and the precariously placed lamps are still in place on their plinths. The body of car 7 ended its days as a shed in Kirkley Run Lowestoft and eventually yielded parts vital to the restoration of car 14.
(East Anglia Transport Museum coll)

55. On the South West corner of the bridge stood a large notice for the attention of all bridge-users and headed Notice. London and North Eastern Railway Byelaws. Did officialdom really expect all these edicts to be fully and universally digested without causing traffic jams additional to those arising from the operation of the bridge? (A.D. Packer coll)

56. In this view of the bridge, from about 1930, eleven means of transport can be seen (just): motor car, motor lorry, motor cycle (and side car), motor bus, railway wagon, sailing craft, hand cart, sack barrow, bicycle, shoe leather and, of course, tram. The ladder backed top deck seats are well portrayed. The bridge semaphore signal is hiding behind the nearest traction pole (left).
(P.Jenkins coll)

PIER TERRACE

57. The photographer seems to have used the balcony of the Harbour Hotel to capture this view of the tramway opening procession passing into Pier Terrace from the bridge. The gentlemen with the extending ladder are probably in attendance in case of mishaps with the technicalities of the bridge over head and not to paint the traction columns which are not yet wearing their top coats. The traffic makes an interesting contrast with that in the previous view. (P. Jenkins coll)

Lowestoft.

A letter soon Best love Alice

58. From ground level, the same location is depicted on this post card shortly after. The area between here and the pier was a good place to pick up a landau and, in later years, a charabanc or motor coach. Perhaps Alice's promised letter related the story of the ride she took. The attractive cottages to the right were demolished when a replacement (bascule) bridge was installed on a more easterly alignment in 1972. (National Tramway Museum coll)

59. An unidentified single deck car awaits the right of way from Pier Terrace and across the bridge. A mother and child have taken advantage of the droplight facility of the window to take some fresh air while their journey is interrupted.
(I. G. Robb Photographic Archive)

60. Passengers are here boarding a north-bound car 12 at the same point on Pier Terrace in the late 1920s. Others waiting to travel south stand by the shelter seen in the next picture. The bridge semaphore signal can be seen by the coal office (right). In the overhead wiring is the section insulator beyond which the overhead supply was de-energised when the bridge was open to shipping. (A. D. Packer)

61. The octagonal passenger refuge was built around a traction column at the Pier Terrace stop in 1904. A similar structure was provided at North Parade, shortly after. (see picture 28). Car 1 has the same dent in its dash plate as is seen in picture 19, in which it is at the southern end of the tram. Turning around of cars occurred as they were deployed from the depot to either north or south over the triangular junction by the Central Station. The Harbour Hotel survives but is now styled the Harbour Inn.
(P. Larter coll)

62. In this 1920s scene, bystanders have about them an air of accustomed resignation which suggests that the bridge is open to shipping and all traffic brought to a halt. Meanwhile, the decorated tram is beginning to lose its novelty appeal. It appears to be the same car as in pictures 96 and 97.
(P. Rasbery coll)

63. A crossover was installed at Pier Terrace from the outset of operations. This enabled cars to make short workings on the south of the system in the event of prolonged opening or mechanical failure of the swing bridge.. (Author's coll)

64.   Car 6 draws our vision beyond the crossover and into London Road South in this pre World War I scene which is full of well portrayed detail. St John's Church is a particularly striking feature. It was a gift to the town by Sir Samuel Morton Peto in 1853. The townscape was diminished by its demolition in 1978. Sheltered housing now occupies the site. (National Tramway Museum coll)

65. In this 1927 view, evening light silhouettes a car passing the corner of Belvedere Road. To the left can be seen the canopy of the 1913 Palace Cinema which was demolished following a fire in 1971. (LCC Tramways Trust coll)

66. Car 6 enters our view of the same location as perceived from the west side pavement but nearly a quarter century before the date of the previous picture. A tramway section box (extreme right) is just one item of street furniture and activity including a postman emptying a pillar box. London Road South stretches into the distance. (East Anglia Transport Museum coll)

LONDON ROAD SOUTH

67. The 1931 demolition gang are here seen removing the track near St Johns Church while filling for the new road surface is catching up with them. The overhead remains in place as does the advertisement for Central Garage fixed to the column. This is one of a number installed by the Standard Illuminated Sign Company. The traction standard can look forward to a new career in street lighting. (C.Wilson coll)

68. Flood waters in January 1905 cover the northern end of London Road South. "Winter" car 21 and a double deck car stand in the dry while crew and onlookers no doubt debate the wisdom or otherwise of taking the plunge. The large terraces have since been thinned out as this formerly residential stretch of road has become more commercial. The former Playhouse in its modern guise as the Hollywood Cinema today enlivens the scene to the extreme right. (P. Rasbery coll)

69. Tracks and overhead are here seen as we look south from near the corner of Windsor Road where Edgars premises are prominent. The tram in the distance is close to the junction of Mill Road where the proposed trolleybus route would have joined the tramway main line. (P. Killby coll)

70. The Mayor has an excuse to pump the foot gong, as a young lad dashes across the path of the opening procession. The tram is just passing the entry to Union Place behind the three storey building (left) which was to become Stead & Simpson's shop in later years. The modern scene is relatively unchanged. An inelegant steel traffic sign gantry which arched the road at this point has since come and, thankfully, gone. (P. Larter coll)

71. From a sight of the first car, we move on to one of the last. The driver doffs his cap in respectful salute as car 2 waits by the stop just north of the Carlton Road / Cliff Road junction. At its steepest point by the actual crossroads, this was the most demanding incline on the system (1 in 27). The proposed line in Ravine Score would have been considerably more taxing and calling for use of the track brakes with which this car was originally fitted.
(East Anglia Transport Museum coll)

72. A car has just passed the corner of Kendal Road (left) and the distinctive lych gate and lodge of Kirkley Cemetery (right). Apart from the modern levels of traffic and the number of parked vehicles, the scene is relatively unchanged today. (P. Rasbery coll)

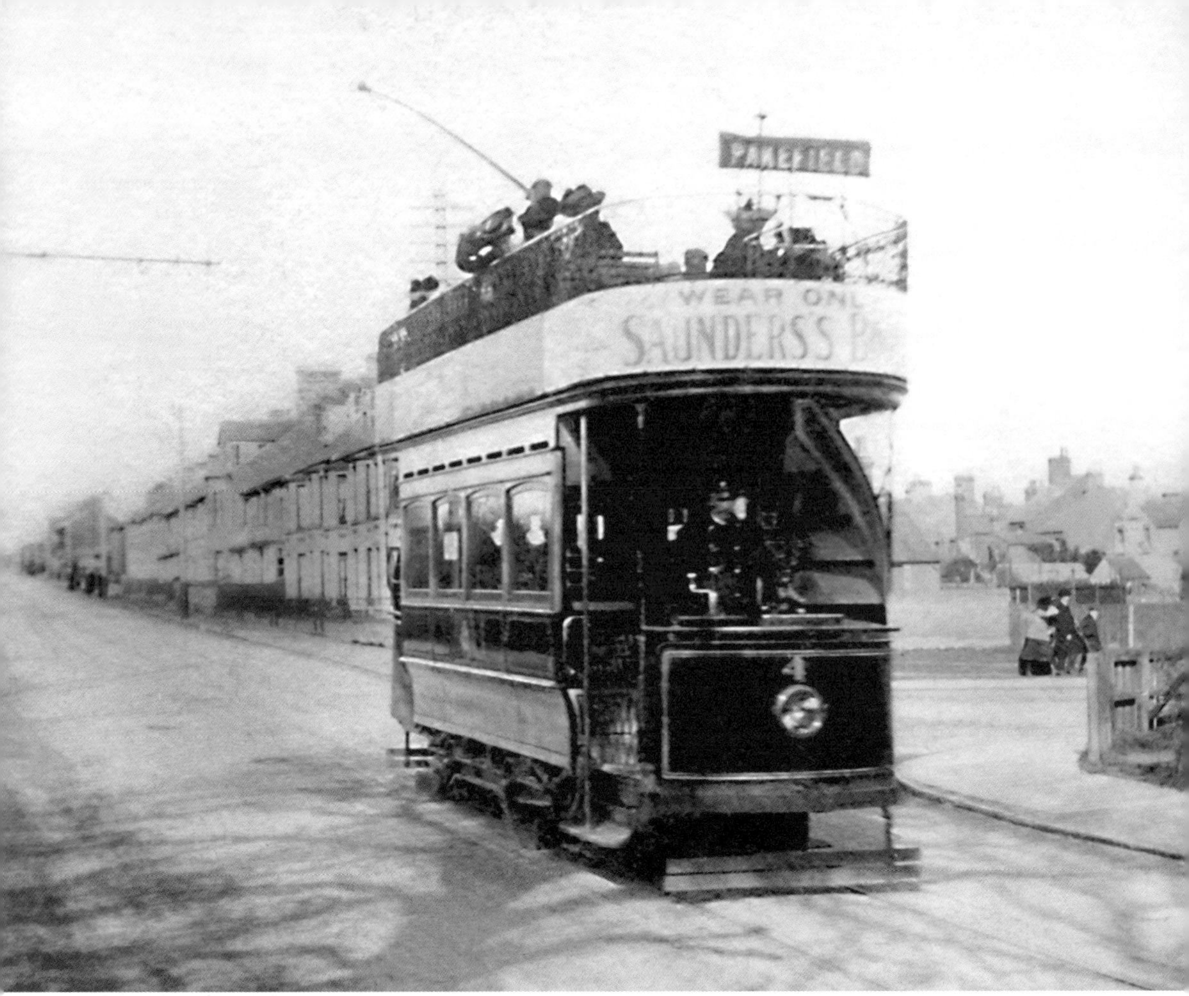
PAKEFIELD
WEAR ONL
SAUNDERS'S B

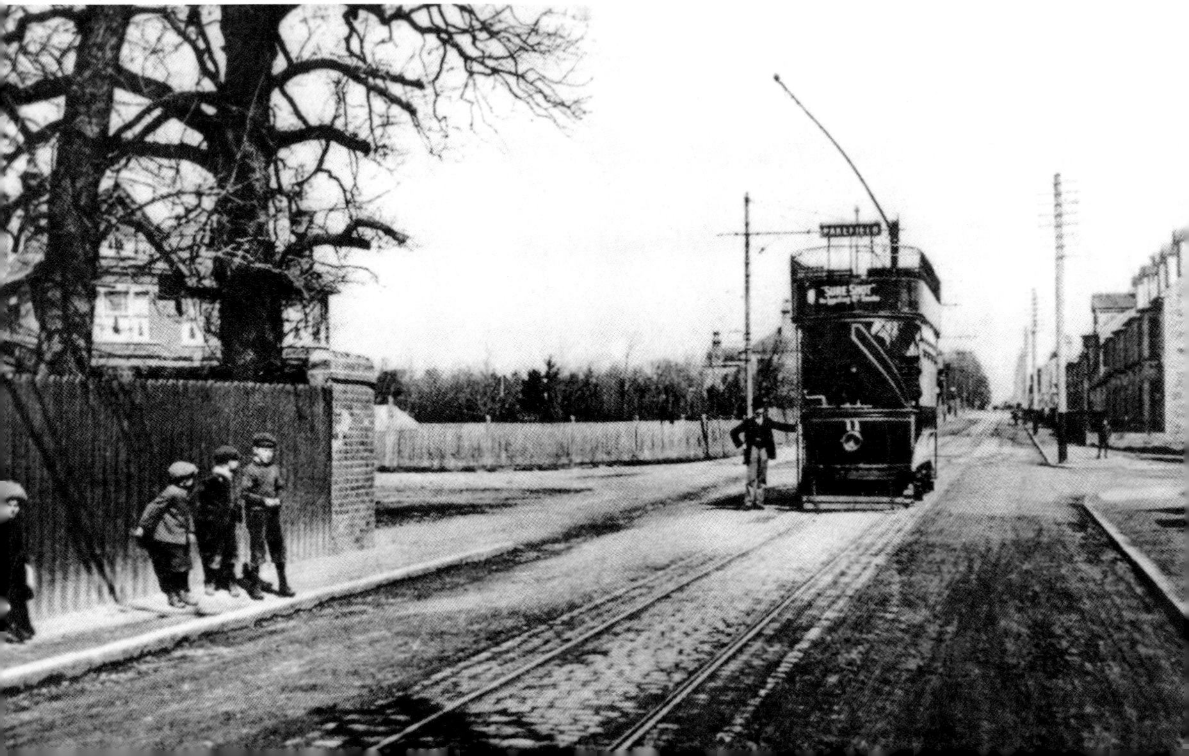
PAKEFIELD
SURE SHOT

← 73. Car 4 passes the point where Short Street and Church Road form a combined junction with London Road South. Church Road has since been renamed All Saints Road. (P. Rasbery coll)

← 74. A gentleman in a bowler hat adopts a proprietorial pose with car 11 which is stopped across the junction of Acton Road (left) and Church Road (right). No doubt he hopes the photographer will get a Sure Shot in concurrence with the advertising on the tram. The children delay their dash across the road until photographer and subject are done. (East Anglia Transport Museum coll)

75. A little further south, we see the bare trees in the previous picture in full leaf. The date is known to be 29th July 1912, when a number of photographs were taken of the installation of underground domestic electricity supply cables (right). Car 24 is seen heading north. After withdrawal, it was cut into at least 2 parts; one of which ended its days as a shed on a small holding at Barnby. (East Anglia Transport Museum coll)

PAKEFIELD

76. At last, we arrive at Pakefield, where Car 4 illustrates the appearance of the cars following World War I when a utility unlined livery was adopted. Certainly, car 4 looks dowdy here by comparison with its original turnout depicted in picture 102. Local subscription libraries like that advertised by Jarrolds have since virtually disappeared. They were the video hire shops of the time. The freehold site to the right was about to become a garage and petrol station. (Photographer unknown. Print courtesy of Suffolk Record Office, Lowestoft Branch)

77. Originally the Corporation's tracks extended beyond the end of Pakefield Street to a terminal stub in front of the Tramway Hotel (right). This piece of road was in the then quite separate parish of Pakefield. The boundary ran down the centre of Pakefield Street (behind the wagon - centre right). In 1912, the Tramways Committee resolved to remove the infrastructure outside the Borough. Among the savings was the annual sum of £5. 13s. 0d (£5.65) rates to the Pakefield authorities. Three years after the closure of the tramways, the whole of Pakefield was absorbed into Lowestoft Borough. (P. Killby coll)

78. Car 1 stands briefly on the original Pakefield terminal stub outside the Tramway Hotel before moving back to the passenger stop at the corner of Stradbroke Road. The Hotel still trades under the same name. A balconied covered topped double decker is now depicted on the sign. No such trams ran in Lowestoft but the Corporation did consider buying some. However, the Board of Trade may not have sanctioned the use of such cars on the exposed narrow gauge track across the swing bridge. (East Anglia Transport Museum coll)

79. Car 10 is seen at the same location but photographed from the eastern side of the road. This is an arrival rather than pre departure photograph. The ladies on top have presumably been persuaded to wait until the photographer has finished before disembarking. The cottages in the background survive today as small shops but the wall to the left has been demolished to make way for the third part of a triangular road layout. (East Anglia Transport Museum coll)

1927 map

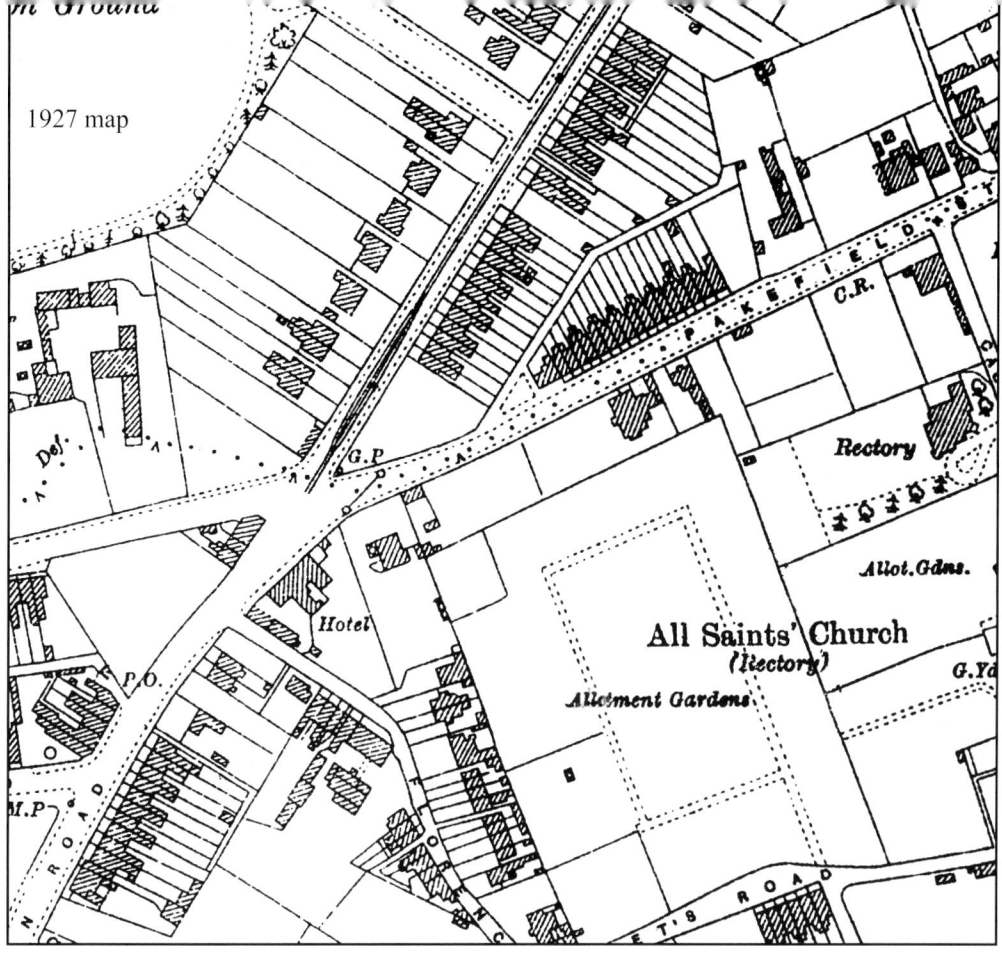

80. Back at the post- 1912 Pakefield terminus by the corner of Stradbroke Road we encounter Corporation motor bus no. 3 (RT 4656); one of three 26 seat Guy BBs with locally built Waveney bodies delivered in 1928. Bus journeys, extended to the North Borough boundary, were inserted into the tram schedules. The first withdrawals of tramcars also occurred in 1928. The red and yellow tramcar livery was retained for the buses until the late 1930s when the dark maroon and primrose colours were adopted. (LCC Tramways Trust coll)

ROTTERDAM ROAD DEPOT

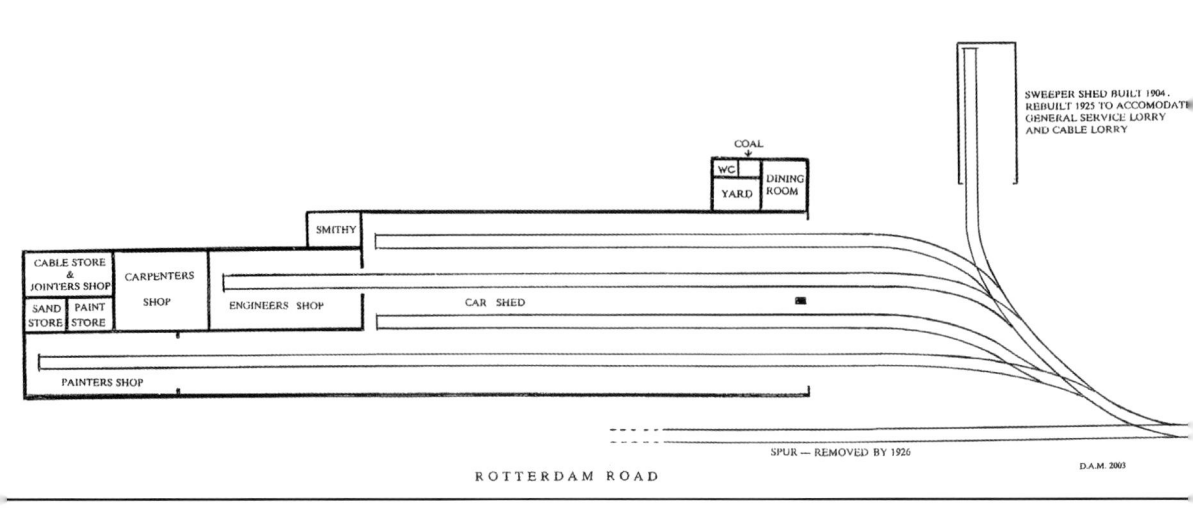

```
                                              COAL
                                               ↓
                                          WC
                                               DINING
                                         YARD  ROOM
                         SMITHY
  CABLE STORE
      &         CARPENTERS
 JOINTERS SHOP    SHOP
                         ENGINEERS SHOP       CAR SHED
  SAND   PAINT
  STORE  STORE

  PAINTERS SHOP

                                                    SPUR — REMOVED BY 1926
                         ROTTERDAM ROAD                              D.A.M. 2003
```

SWEEPER SHED BUILT 1904.
REBUILT 1925 TO ACCOMODATE
GENERAL SERVICE LORRY
AND CABLE LORRY

81. Rotterdam Road depot is seen here shortly before the opening of the system in July 1903. The trucks of three cars yet to be assembled stand on the depot fan. The paving of this area was still not complete at the commencement of services.
(Tramway & Railway World / East Anglia Transport Museum)

82. All had been tidied up when this picture was taken. The three cars to the left are standing on the road leading to the paint shop. Access to the engineers' shop is behind the single deck car centre right. The horse drawn tower wagon was replaced by another heavier one following an accident in March 1904 when it overturned injuring 2 tramway employees and a pedestrian.
(National Tramway Museum coll)

83. Quite what is happening here to car 5 is not recorded. Although the packing looks precarious, the weight distribution in the design of the tram precludes its falling to our left. Orthodox methods of tram repair entailed use of the extensive depot pits between the rails or jacks and lifting beams.
(East Anglia
Transport Museum coll)

POWER GENERATION

84.	Inside the generating station, we see some of the additional plant that was installed to provide power to the tramways. To the left is a Lancashire Dynamo and Motor Co. generator. The engine in the centre is a Willans and Robinson three crank compound while that beyond is a two crank compound by Browett and Lindley. (Tramway & Railway World)

85. The main switchboard was supplied by the British Westinghouse Company. The equipment was mounted on 6 marble panels and controlled the distribution of power to the tramway system through four feeder pillars and six section pillars located at various points along the route.
(Tramway and Railway World / National Tramway Museum)

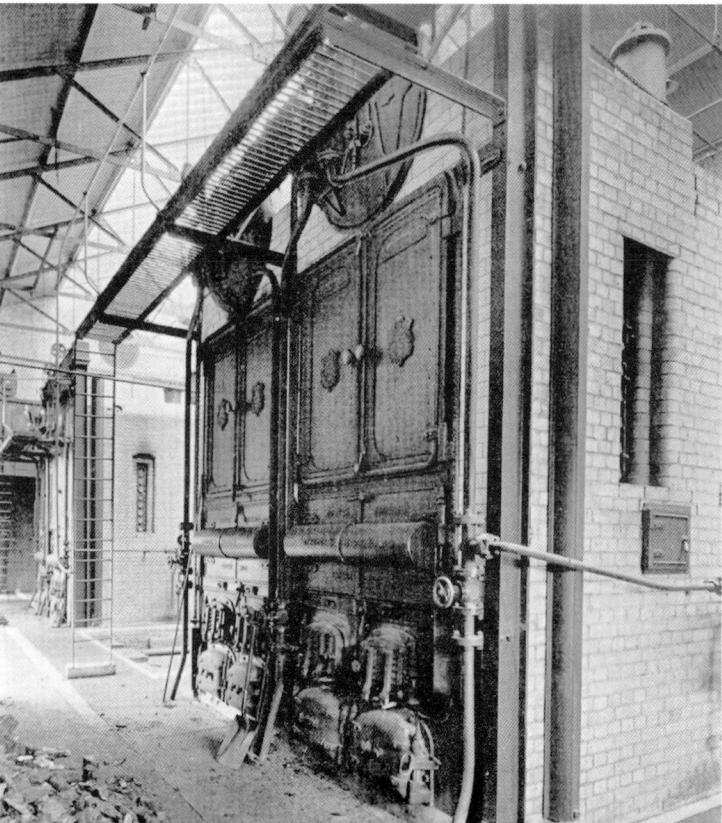

86. The generating station boiler room contained four Babcock and Wilcox water tube boilers pressed to 160lb per square inch. The temporarily rested shovel and the pile of coal testify to the fact that fuelling these boilers was originally by good old hard graft. An overhead conveyor system was installed in the 1920s.
(Tramway and Railway World / National Tramway Museum)

87. Electric traction came to the railways in 1912 in the form of a powered rope shunting capstain in the Corporation's coal receiving sidings just to the northwest of Coke Ovens Junction. The tracks seen curving to the right crossed Denmark Road and the electric tramway on the level to access a long siding terminating by the power station. (Reproduced from the Lowestoft Borough Archives, courtesy of Waveney District Council)

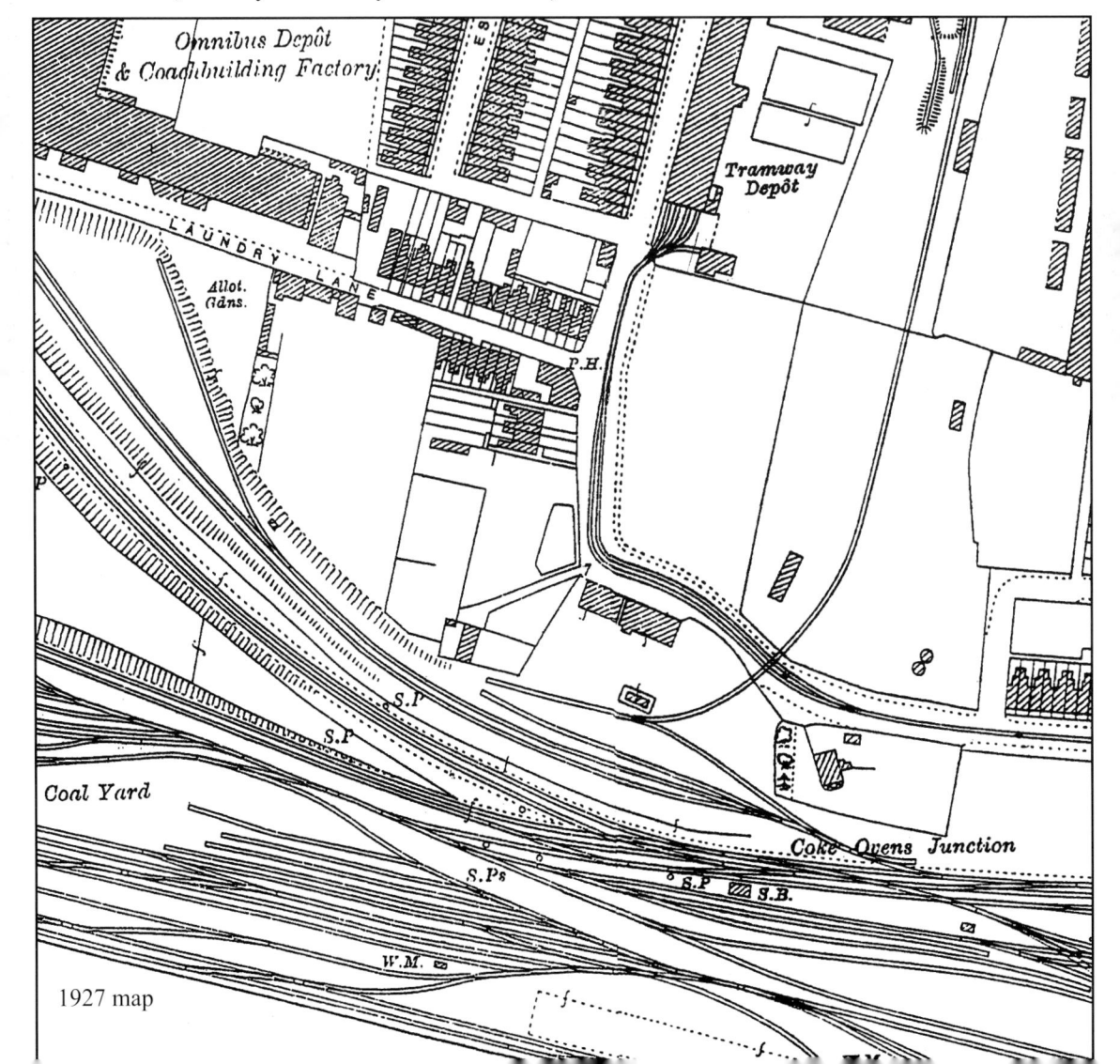

1927 map

TRAMWAY PEOPLE

88. A group of crews and other staff pose in front of one of the new 1904 cars. In the background is Rotterdam Road and behind the tram is a column supporting the overhead for the wiring above the spur which originally ran in this road and along the side of the depot. (P. Killby coll)

89. James (Sunny Jim) Friston obviously felt sufficiently proud of his conductor's uniform and white summer cap cover to take himself to the local photographer. He retired after 38 years service; latterly as a diligent bus inspector known to crews as "The High Street Ghost". (D. Friston coll)

Like many other undertakings, the Lowestoft tramways recruited women during the First World War to cover duties of male employees serving in the forces. Less common was the retention from 1916 onwards of women as drivers although this was to become more widespread elsewhere during World War II. Altogether, 75 women helped with the running of the tramways during hostilities. Of these, 17 served as drivers and 2 as inspectors.

90. General Manager Herbert Saunders and two of his inspectors (Peck, left and Strowger, right) are seen here with a group of clippies, taken on to replace crewmen serving with the armed forces in 1915. The clippie front right is known to be Miss Charlish (later Mrs Wernham), who subsequently became a driver.(F. Wernham coll)

91. Driver Louise Shipp (later Gowing) and Olive Bately (later Utting) stand with a rather battered bogie car 22 at Pakefield. There was no love lost between Miss Shipp and this particular car. She recounted an incident in the blackout, when 22 repeatedly split the depot points in an attempt to enter the building sideways! (East Anglia Transport Museum coll)

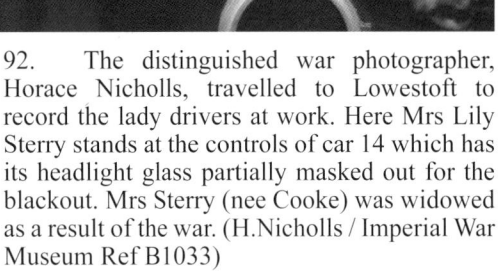

92. The distinguished war photographer, Horace Nicholls, travelled to Lowestoft to record the lady drivers at work. Here Mrs Lily Sterry stands at the controls of car 14 which has its headlight glass partially masked out for the blackout. Mrs Sterry (nee Cooke) was widowed as a result of the war. (H.Nicholls / Imperial War Museum Ref B1033)

93. Three members of the operating staff were awarded the Military Medal during World War I including J Crickmore (driver), and W. Bemment · (Inspector) ·left. The latter wears his MM and campaign ribands on his tunic. The author has been unable to determine whether or not the conductor is the third MM recipient· H. Clarke.
(East Anglia Transport Museum coll)

In 1919, female operating staff organised a dinner to welcome home from the war the active service employees. The Menu obviously formed part of the evening's entertainment! By way of commemoration, the back page listed the eleven men who were absent; having made the Supreme Sacrifice.

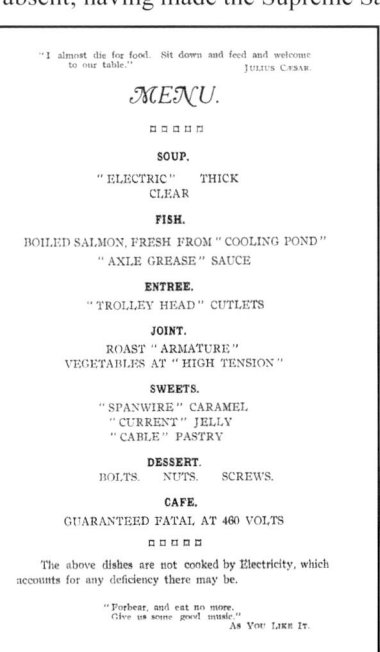

LOWESTOFT CORPORATION ELECTRICITY & TRAMWAYS DEPT
DINNER AT ROYAL HOTEL
TO WELCOME HOME
ACTIVE SERVICE EMPLOYEES
THURSDAY MAY 15 1919 7.0 PM

"I almost die for food. Sit down and feed and welcome to our table."
JULIUS CÆSAR.

MENU.

□ □ □ □ □

SOUP.
"ELECTRIC" THICK
CLEAR

FISH.
BOILED SALMON, FRESH FROM "COOLING POND"
"AXLE GREASE" SAUCE

ENTREE.
"TROLLEY HEAD" CUTLETS

JOINT.
ROAST "ARMATURE"
VEGETABLES AT "HIGH TENSION"

SWEETS.
"SPANWIRE" CARAMEL
"CURRENT" JELLY
"CABLE" PASTRY

DESSERT.
BOLTS. NUTS. SCREWS.

CAFE.
GUARANTEED FATAL AT 460 VOLTS

□ □ □ □ □

The above dishes are not cooked by Electricity, which accounts for any deficiency there may be.

"Forbear, and eat no more,
Give us some good music."
AS YOU LIKE IT.

HIGH DAYS AND HOLIDAYS

94.   A church or Sunday school outing is the probable occasion as two 1903 cars loaded to the gunwhales stand at the Pakefield terminus in about 1906.(J. Holmes coll)

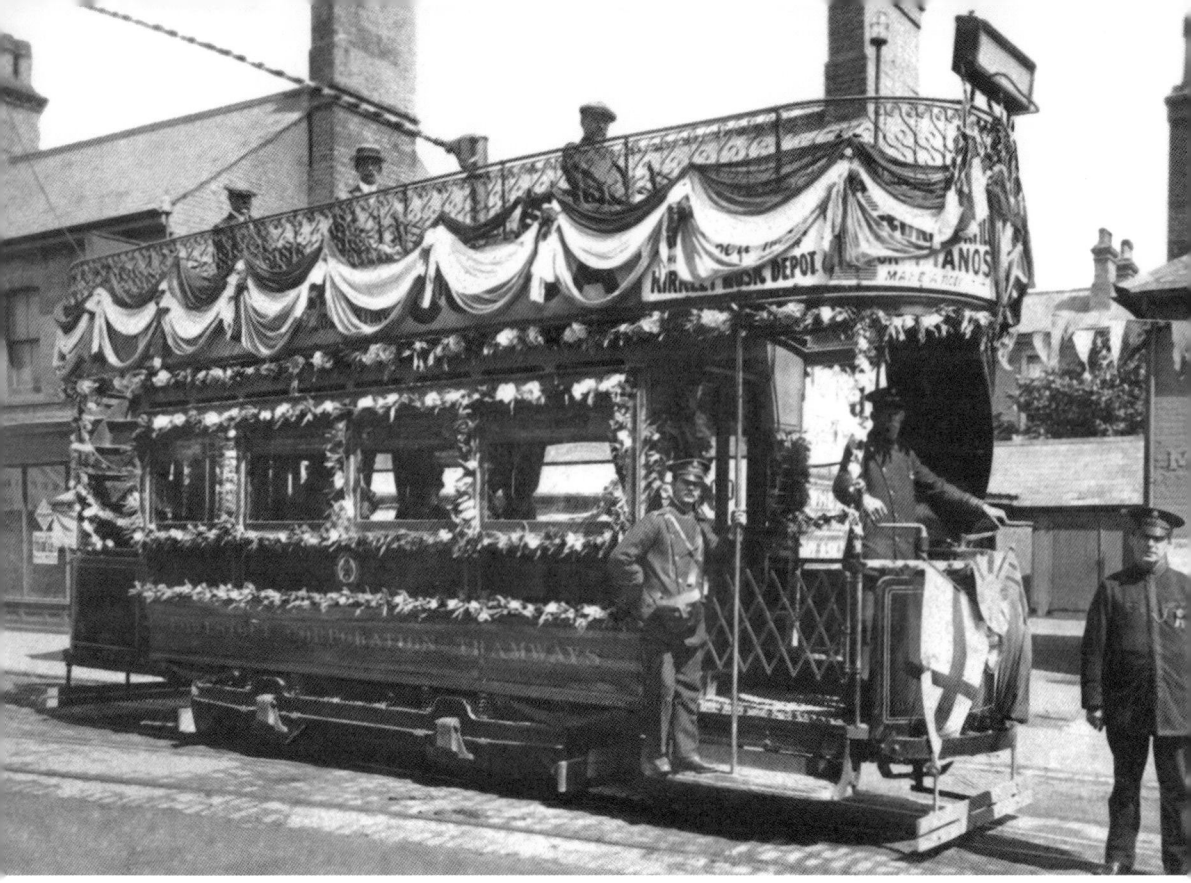

95. This 1903 car is one of those decorated for the 1911 Coronation of King George V at a cost of £12 8s 9d (£12.43). Driver George Warnes and colleagues have posed their car by the Plough and Sail public house (extreme right), just north of Claremont Road in London Road South. (East Anglia Transport Museum coll)

← 96. The flags for this 1920s turnout would be appropriate for Empire day. Manager Herbert Saunders stands in the fore-ground while Inspectors Garrard and Bemment attend at the rear. Mr. Saunders succeeded the original manager, Mr. Bruce, in 1913.
(East Anglia Transport Museum coll)

97. What appears to be the same car is photographed at the eastern end of Denmark Road and near the Central railway station. The driver's view to the left was restricted on Lowestoft cars by the presence of the (reversed) staircase. The decorators have here managed to balance up that deficiency on the right; leaving only a modicum of forward vision available.
(East Anglia Transport Museum coll)

98. If passengers are permitted on this tram they must run the risk of being shanghaied! This oriental pagoda is based on a double deck car with top deck seats and railings removed. Two of the staff travelling incognito are known to be Joe Crack; driver (centre) and Chief Inspector Sidney Garrard (right). The occasion is the 1924 carnival and the location is Pakefield terminus. (East Anglia Transport Museum coll)

99. East meets east? Conductor (dressed in Asian attire) and driver Shiner Wright (turned out as a Suffolk yokel) are caught by the camera at Pakefield terminus during another carnival week. (East Anglia Transport Museum coll)

PERMANENT WAY

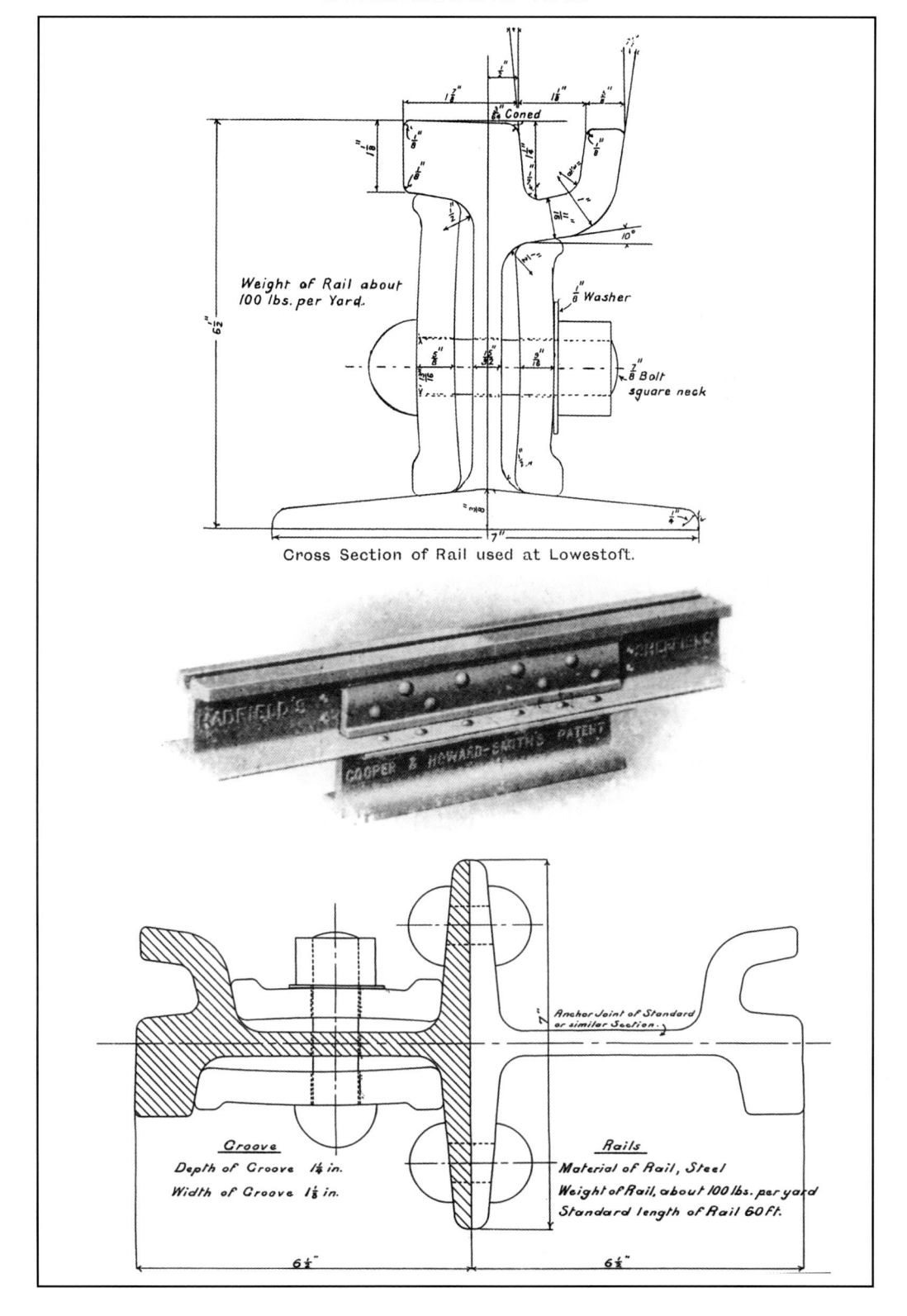

Weight of Rail about 100 lbs. per Yard.

Cross Section of Rail used at Lowestoft.

Groove
Depth of Groove 1¼ in.
Width of Groove 1⅛ in.

Rails
Material of Rail, Steel
Weight of Rail, about 100 lbs. per yard
Standard length of Rail 60 ft.

The 3ft 6ins (1067mm) gauge track was laid using 100 lb grooved rail originally supplied from the Belgian factory of Marcinelli Cauillet by Alexander Penny & Co.

This was laid on a 6ins (152mm) concrete bed and paved with basaltic lava blocks edged with blocks of granite; subsequently replaced by granite setts and, in places, by jarrah blocks.

The lava was chosen because of its noiselessness and non slip quality but proved not to be durable. Water penetrated the formation and damaged the foundations which had to be renewed. The rails were joined with Cooper and Howard Smith's anchor joints. Points and special work were provided by Hadfields of Sheffield.

100. The special trackwork for the railway and tramway crossing by Waveney Road is here seen laid out before delivery at Hadfield & Co's Sheffield works. The narrow gauge tramway double track is seen top to bottom and the wider (standard gauge) railway track from left to right. The pointwork (top right to bottom left) was to cater for a tramway extension via Waveney Road which was never built. Other special work was ordered to provide for another line from the Central Station into Bevan Street which was also never constructed.
(Tramway & Railway World/National Tramway Museum)

101. The special work in the previous picture is seen shortly after installation and before being paved. Central station is in the background and there is an interesting looking tank wagon in a siding. (Author's coll)

ROLLING STOCK

All passenger cars were supplied by the British Westinghouse Electric and Manufacturing Company and incorporated their type 46, 25HP motors and model 90 controllers. The construction of the cars themselves was sub-contracted to G.F. Milnes & Company of Hadley, Shropshire.

Double deck cars 1-11 1903

These four wheeled open top cars seated 22 passengers on longitudinal wooden seats in the saloon and 26 on reversible ladder back seats on the top deck. The saloons had four arched windows each side which could be lowered for extra ventilation. Inside, the roof was of the monitor type·an internal clerestory. The ceilings were decorated with birdseye maple enhanced with elaborate lining and motifs. The trim was a combination of mahogany, oak, ash and sequoia. The staircases were of the reversed (clockwise) type.. The six foot (1.8m) wheelbase trucks were described as Milnes girder type, but were actually fabricated by WCF Busch of Bautzen, Germany. Milnes had effectively become a subsidiary of Busch in 1898.

As constructed, these cars were fitted with track brakes controlled by a hand wheel fitted around the hand brake shaft. These brakes were soon removed with the evident exception of those on car 3 which, presumably, doubled as a rail grinder. During the World War I, the roller blind route indicators were replaced with boards affixed to the centre window pillars. In 1921, these boards were turned over to advertising. At about the same time, decorative wrought iron work around the top deck railings was replaced with galvanised wire mesh.

Single deck ("winter") cars 21-24 1903

These unusual cars were narrow gauge versions of 5 similar standard gauge cars, built in 1902 for the Gateshead and District Tramways Company. As built, they seated 26 passengers on transverse reversible seats in a central saloon and 6 each in semi open smokers' compartments at the ends.. The gangway clearance was just 15ins (383mm). In 1904, longitudinal seating was substitued in the saloons and the end compartments enclosed. Longitudinal seats were fitted throughout in 1910. These cars were equipped with Busch maximum traction bogies which were inclined to derail. Consequently, they saw considerably less use than the double deckers. (There is a reference in the 1903 Tramway Committee minutes to the bogey cars; a Freudian slip, no doubt!. In the same vein is a much later reference to electrical equipment from Metropolitan Vicars!)

As with the double deckers, the saloon windows could be lowered and trim materials were the same. Track brakes were originally fitted and subsequently removed.

Double deck cars 12-15 1904

Having considered and ruled out closed top balcony double deckers the Corporation decided to order 4 more cars of the 1 - 11 pattern from Milnes. However, these cars were never fitted with track brakes and differed from the 1903 cars in other small details including livery and trim. Subsequent modifications were the same as in the case of the 1903 cars. The Milnes factory closed later in 1904.

Livery

The original colours were Munich Lake (a brownish red) and cream. The lake was applied to waist level panels, staircases, dash panels and cantrails. Areas painted cream were rocker (lower) panels, saloon sides and ends above the waist and, in the case of single deck cars, the roof. Fenders and platform steps were black.

Trucks and running gear were red; almost certainly red oxide, eventually. Lake areas were lined with a half inch line of gold leaf and a white line arranged in panels on the car sides with dagger motifs in the corners. The cream was lined boldly in black and more subtly in places in red. Lettering was gold shaded blue and silver. The original emblem was a representation of the Borough seal and placed mid way along the waist panels. Doors and window frames were varnished wood.

A rich shade of yellow had replaced the cream by about 1910; other details remaining unchanged. During World War I, a utility livery without lining was resorted to for the double deckers. Subsequently, a simplified full livery was adopted in which plain yellow replaced the gold leaf lining and without motifs. The Borough's armorial bearings replaced the old depiction of the Borough seal.

Because of their relatively limited use, the single deck cars appear to have been revarnished rather than fully repainted and to have retained their gold leaf lining until withdrawn. Over the years, the lake red will have taken on a progressively darker hue.

Sweeper car (un-numbered) 1903

This was the most substantial such car supplied to any East Anglian tramway system. Available details are limited and only one photograph could be found by the author. It was obviously falling into disfavour by 1913 when the Corporation was seeking to exchange it for something more suitable. Subsequent history cannot be traced. The car was supplied by Brecknell, Munro and Rogers of Bristol and mounted on Brush reversed maximum traction trucks. As delivered it was painted grey.

When additional depot space was needed for the new double deckers in 1904, a separate shed was built for the sweeper. (See depot plan)

Rail grinder

Hardly a car, this appliance consisted of grinding gear chain driven by an electric motor mounted on a simple frame with a wheelbase of 4 feet (1220 mm). It was designed to be towed.

Withdrawal dates

No records of the withdrawal of individual cars are known to survive. It is believed that sale of double deck car bodies began early in 1931 as the fleet was reduced in advance of the closure of the system.

Of the four single deckers, two bodies are known to have been released for sale in 1928. (numbers not recorded)

Dimensions

See drawings. Possibly because of an inaccurate press release, some incorrect data appeared in the technical journals in 1903 and reappeared in subsequent publications. Dimensions shown are from Milnes drawings and surviving car bodies.

102. This postcard published to commemorate the opening of the tramways depicts a brand new car 4 at the Belle Vue terminus. No 4 typifies the first 11 double deckers (numbered 1-11) delivered in 1903 in all their original finery. Also depicted are two heroes of the tramways. Lancelot Orde as Mayor and Chairman of the Tramways Committee provided the political drive and energy to bring the tramways into being. Mr. W. G. Bruce was the original Tramways Manager and also Borough Electrical Engineer. Something of an innovator; his ambitions to expand and develop the tramways were frustrated by the Corporation's understandably cautious approach to incurring more debt. (A Brotchie coll)

103. Car 2 of the 1903 batch is just over halfway through its service life as it is seen here approaching the bridge from the south; not long after World War I. It is in largely original condition apart from the removal of track brakes and route indicators. It wears the unlined war time livery. Bovril is advertised above the canopy. This was issued to fortify the crews against winter conditions during and following the war. (Jack Herd coll)

104. The platform of Car 2 looks a sorry sight on the morning after the night before. The damage was sustained in car 2's role as the very last tram to run on the night of 8th May 1931. (see picture 120) The lattice gate has yielded to passenger pressure and the brake handle has disappeared. (East Anglia Transport Museum coll)

105. For a while, a tramway postal service was provided with posting boxes slung over the dash top rail and fastened to the fender. In this posed picture of car 10 are conductor Freddie Reynolds, driver Harvey Crawford and tramway maintenance man Charlie Holman. Last post in 1930 was by trams leaving the termini just after 8pm. (East Anglia Transport Museum coll)

106. Car 10 again demonstrates another and earlier use for the fender ie. to advertise summer shows at the Sparrows Nest Theatre. The show So This Is Romance ran during the last week of July 1927. In the 1920s, many cars had their dash plates repaired with a linear patch as illustrated here. (A.V. Bird coll)

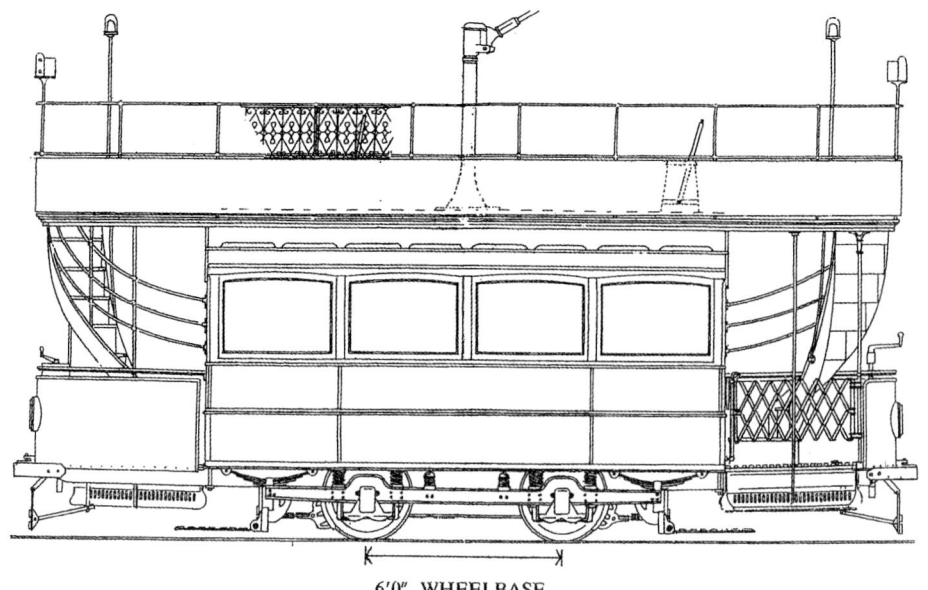

6' 0" WHEELBASE

LENGTH OF BODY 16' 0"

OVERALL LENGTH 27' 8"

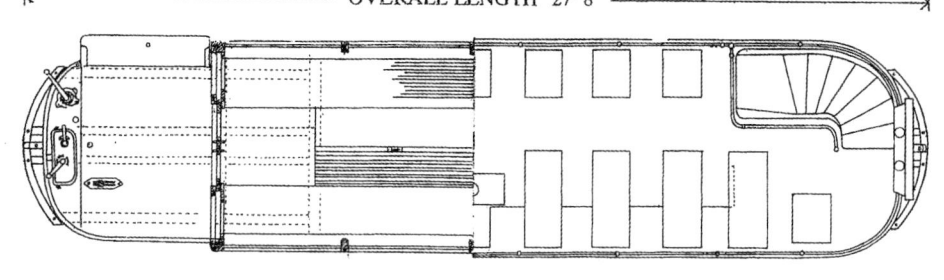

LOWER DECK 22 SEATS   UPPER DECK 26 SEATS

1904
Double Deck car

D.A.M. 2009

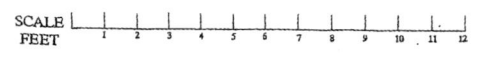

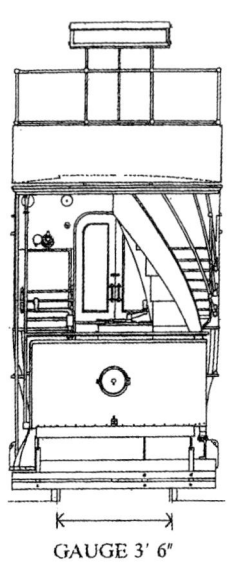

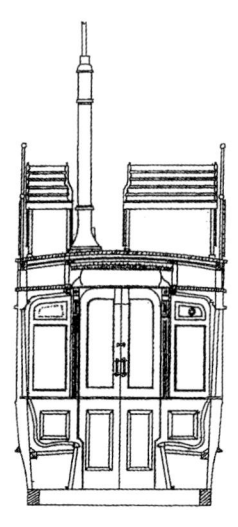

SCALE FEET 1 2 3 4 5 6 7 8 9 10 11 12

GAUGE 3' 6"

6' 2½" OVER PILLARS

107. Car 14 was one of the batch of 4 double deckers (numbered 12-15) added to the fleet in 1904. These cars were without track brakes from the outset and there were other relatively minor differences of detail with the earlier cars. It is seen here at the North Station when still relatively new and in what were then very rural surroundings. (Jack Herd coll)

108. The interior of car 14 is seen at the East Anglia Transport Museum and before full restoration began. The glazed louvres in the roof emitted little or no day light but matched the clerestory lights of the single deck cars. (Author)

109. As a first step towards the tram's re-incarnation, the saloon of car 14 is rescued from its retirement life as part of a bungalow at Middle Drive, Gunton on 23rd April 1962. (Author)

110. During the 1960s and 1970s, Car 14 was reconstructed; although not to full working order, under the leadership of Mr A. V. (Dick) Bird who is seen here with the recreated car at the East Anglia Transport Museum. As this book goes to press, the long process of totally rebuilding 14 to operating condition is under way. (M Vickers)

↗ 111. The four distinctive, but somewhat disappointing single deck cars (numbered 21 -24), only ran in this condition very briefly. Advertisment panels were soon fitted above each cantrail. More fundamentally, the semi enclosed end smoking compartments were glazed and panelled after about a year.
(Tramway & Railway World /
East Anglia Transport Museum)

4' 0" WHEELBASE

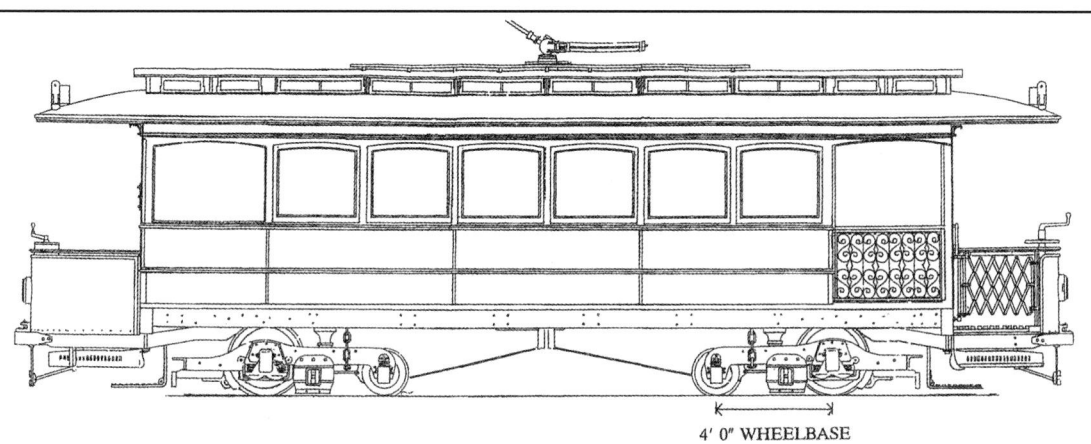

LENGTH OF BODY 28' 0"

OVERALL LENGTH 36' 6"

END COMPARTMENT 6 SEATS

MAIN SALOON 26 SEATS

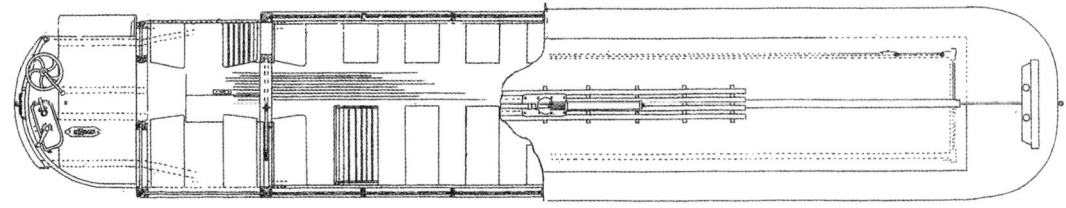

6' 2½" OVER PILLARS

Single deck car as built

D.A.M. 2009

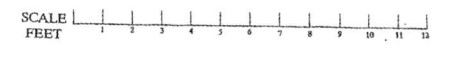

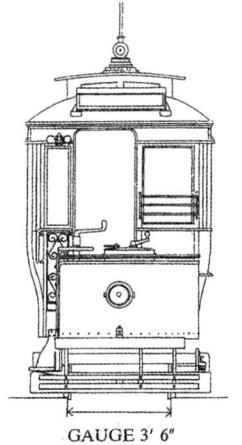

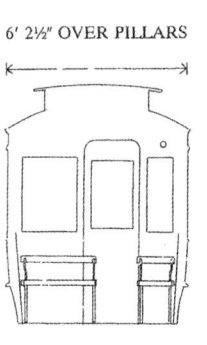

SCALE FEET 1 2 3 4 5 6 7 8 9 10 11 12

GAUGE 3' 6"

112. The appearance of the bogie cars had something of a North American flavour. The impression is amplified on this example by an item of spelling in the advertising. In fact, partially open single deckers of this general style were sometimes called California Cars in tramway circles. Combination Car was the official term. Car 22 is seen here, probably at Pakefield, in 1903/4. (A. Brotchie coll)

113. No longer technically a combination, this unidentifiable bogie car is seen on Yarmouth Road after the enclosure of the smokers' compartments in 1904. The ornamental grille was panelled over from the inside. Eventually, it was covered externally with flat sheeting with no attempt being made to extend the curved profile of the remainder of the body. The external bulkhead remained doorless throughout but there was a sliding door between the main saloon and each end compartment. Between the bogies are dog guards; fitted in this case following an accident involving a child. The track brakes have been removed. (J.Herd coll)

114. This single decker is at Pier Terrace in the very 1920s. It still carries gold lined livery as these troublesome cars were put to less use than the double deckers and required only periodic varnishing rather than full repainting. The largely vacant framework for all round roof advertising was fitted after route information was transferred to the window ledges. Clearly, advertisers did not want to pay for exposure so often limited to the depot interior. (J.Herd coll)

4' 0" WHEELBASE

LENGTH OF BODY 28' 0"

OVERALL LENGTH 36' 6"

END COMPARTMENT 6 SEATS

MAIN SALOON 26 SEATS

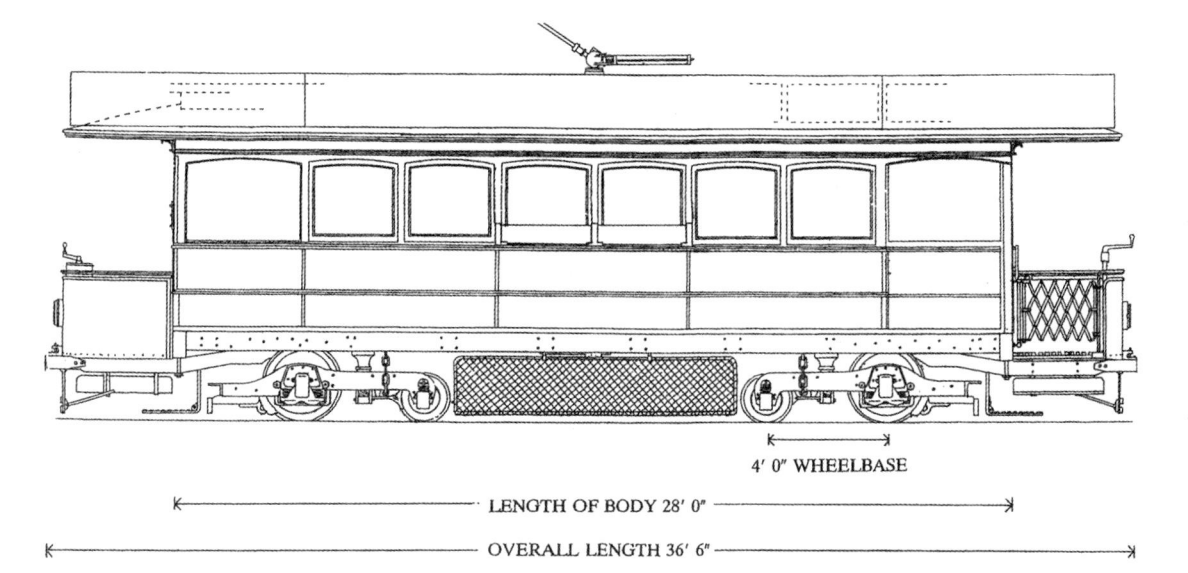

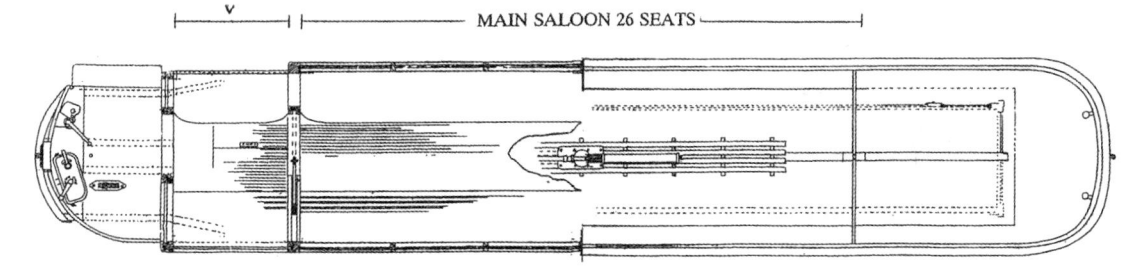

Single deck car as modified

D.A.M. 2009

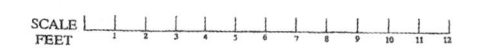

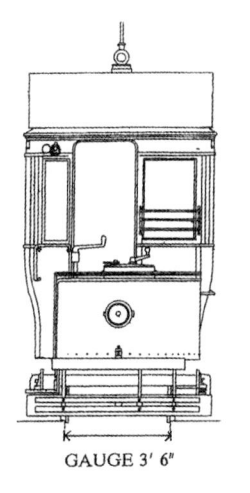

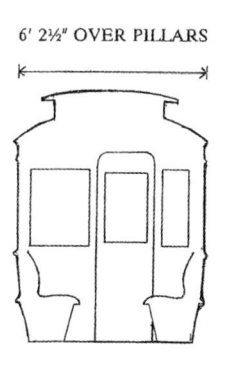

SCALE FEET 1 2 3 4 5 6 7 8 9 10 11 12

6' 2½" OVER PILLARS

GAUGE 3' 6"

115. The body of one single decker (known not to be 24 but as yet unidentified) became part of a bungalow in Blackheath Road, Lowestoft from whence it was removed to the East Anglia Transport Museum in 1990. The pitched roof which it obtained as a residence has been retained for its indefinite outdoor life as an exhibition room. (Author)

116. Although the electric street tramway at Lowestoft was the smallest in East Anglia, it did go in for some things in a big way. No one else in the region had such a water car and track cleaner as this. It was supplied by Brecknell Munro and Rogers on Brush reversed maximum traction trucks. The gentleman at the controls appears to be the mayor; Councillor Orde adopting a Look what we've got! pose for the benefit of other municipalities. (National Tramway Museum coll)

FINALE

117. This scene outside the depot would appear to date from the morning after the closure on 8th May 1931. The rubber tyre on car 2's dash is believed to have been the basis of the wreath seen in the pictures, 71 and 118. The bus is one of 4 Guy FC single deckers with bodies built by United at what was to become Eastern Coach Works; a short walk up Laundry Lane from the left of the picture. Identified individuals are Billy Bellinger (extreme left) and George Baldry (centre left). (East Anglia Transport Museum coll)

The Last Car
Lowestoft

← 118. The wreath of arum lilies worn by the last car throughout 8th May 1931 is depicted in this informal picture taken in Station Square. Sidney Wright stands at the controls and Sidney Poole is second right. (Mrs E. Eade coll)

← 119. This comic card was drawn by Cynicus in or before 1907 and was produced printed with the names of many individual towns so as to have near universal application. Last car in this instance should be taken to mean last service car of the day (or night) but the last car of all invariably also attracted crowds of passengers anxious to be part of a piece of history. (P Killby coll)

120. The last Lowestoft car in reality is seen here at Pier Terrace on the night of 8th May 1931. In the crowd towards the left stands the moustached figure of Lancelot Orde who had been instrumental in setting Lowestoft tram wheels in motion 28 years, eight million miles and eighty million passenger journeys earlier. (B.Gowen coll)

Middleton Press
EVOLVING THE ULTIMATE RAIL ENCYCLOPEDIA

Easebourne Lane, Midhurst, West Sussex.
GU29 9AZ Tel:01730 813169
www.middletonpress.co.uk email:info@middletonpress.co.uk
A-978 0 906520 B- 978 1 873793 C- 978 1 901706 D-978 1 904474 E - 978 1 906008

All titles listed below were in print at time of publication - please check current availability by looking at our website - *www.middletonpress.co.uk* or by requesting a Brochure which includes our LATEST RAILWAY TITLES also our TRAMWAY, TROLLEYBUS, MILITARY and WATERWAYS series

A
Abergavenny to Merthyr C 91 8
Abertillery and Ebbw Vale Lines D 84 5
Allhallows - Branch Line to A 62 8
Alton - Branch Lines to A 11 6
Andover to Southampton A 82 6
Ascot - Branch Lines around A 64 2
Ashburton - Branch Line to B 95 4
Ashford - Steam to Eurostar B 67 1
Ashford to Dover A 48 2
Austrian Narrow Gauge D 04 3
Avonmouth - BL around D 42 5
Aylesbury to Rugby D 91 3

B
Baker Street to Uxbridge D 90 6
Banbury to Birmingham D 27 2
Banbury to Cheltenham E 63 5
Barking to Southend C 80 2
Barmouth to Pwllheli E 53 6
Barry - Branch Lines around D 50 0
Bath Green Park to Bristol C 36 9
Bath to Evercreech Junction A 60 4
Bedford to Wellingborough D 31 9
Birmingham to Wolverhampton E 25 3
Bletchley to Cambridge D 94 4
Bletchley to Rugby E 07 9
Bodmin - Branch Lines around B 83 1
Bournemouth & Poole Trys B 47 3
Bournemouth to Evercreech Jn A 46 8
Bournemouth to Weymouth A 57 4
Brecon to Neath D 43 2
Brecon to Newport D 16 6
Brecon to Newtown E 06 2
Brighton to Eastbourne A 16 1
Brighton to Worthing A 03 1
Bromley South to Rochester B 23 7
Bromsgrove to Birmingham D 87 6
Bromsgrove to Gloucester D 73 9
Brunel - A railtour of his achievements D 74 6
Bude - Branch Line to B 29 9
Burnham to Evercreech Junction B 68 0

C
Cambridge to Ely D 55 5
Canterbury - Branch Lines around B 58 9
Cardiff to Dowlais (Cae Harris) E 47 5
Cardiff to Swansea E 42 0
Carmarthen to Fishguard E 66 6
Caterham & Tattenham Corner B 25 1
Chard and Yeovil - BLs around C 30 7
Charing Cross to Dartford A 75 8
Charing Cross to Orpington A 96 3
Cheddar - Branch Line to B 90 9
Cheltenham to Andover C 43 7
Cheltenham to Redditch D 81 4
Chichester to Portsmouth A 14 7
Clapham Junction to Beckenham Jn B 36 7
Cleobury Mortimer - BLs around E 18 5
Clevedon & Portishead - BLs to D 18 0
Colonel Stephens D 62 3
Consett to South Shields E 57 4
Cornwall Narrow Gauge D 56 2
Corris and Vale of Rheidol E 65 9
Craven Arms to Llandeilo E 35 2
Craven Arms to Wellington E 33 8
Crawley to Littlehampton A 34 5
Cromer - Branch Lines around C 26 0
Croydon to East Grinstead B 48 0
Crystal Palace and Catford Loop B 87 1
Cyprus Narrow Gauge E 13 0

D
Darlington - Leamside - Newcastle E 28 4
Darlington to Newcastle D 98 2
Dartford to Sittingbourne B 34 3
Derwent Valley - Branch Line to the D 06 7
Devon Narrow Gauge E 09 3
Didcot to Banbury D 02 9
Didcot to Swindon C 84 0
Didcot to Winchester C 13 0
Dorset & Somerset Narrow Gauge D 76 2

Douglas to Peel C 88 8
Douglas to Port Erin C 55 0
Douglas to Ramsey D 39 5
Dover to Ramsgate A 78 9
Dublin Northwards in the 1950s E 31 4
Dunstable - Branch Lines to E 27 7

E
Ealing to Slough C 42 0
East Cornwall Mineral Railways D 22 7
East Croydon to Three Bridges A 53 6
Eastern Spain Narrow Gauge E 56 7
East Grinstead - Branch Lines to A 07 9
East London - Branch Lines of C 44 4
East London Line B 80 0
East of Norwich - Branch Lines E 69 7
Effingham Junction - BLs around A 74 1
Ely to Norwich C 90 1
Enfield Town & Palace Gates - BL to D 32 6
Epsom to Horsham A 30 7
Eritrean Narrow Gauge E 38 3
Euston to Harrow & Wealdstone C 89 5
Exeter to Barnstaple B 15 2
Exeter to Newton Abbot C 49 9
Exeter to Tavistock B 69 5
Exmouth - Branch Lines to B 00 8

F
Fairford - Branch Line to A 52 9
Falmouth, Helston & St. Ives - BL to C 74 1
Fareham to Salisbury A 67 3
Faversham to Dover B 05 3
Felixstowe & Aldeburgh - BL to D 20 3
Fenchurch Street to Barking C 20 8
Festiniog - 50 yrs of enterprise C 83 3
Festiniog 1946-55 E 01 7
Festiniog in the Fifties B 68 8
Festiniog in the Sixties B 91 6
Finsbury Park to Alexandra Palace C 02 8
Frome to Bristol B 77 0

G
Gloucester to Bristol D 35 7
Gloucester to Cardiff D 66 1
Gosport - Branch Lines around A 36 9
Greece Narrow Gauge D 72 2

H
Hampshire Narrow Gauge D 36 4
Harrow to Watford D 14 2
Hastings to Ashford A 37 6
Hawkhurst - Branch Line to A 66 6
Hayling - Branch Line to A 12 3
Hay-on-Wye - Branch Lines around D 92 0
Haywards Heath to Seaford A 28 4
Hemel Hempstead - Branch Lines to D 88 3
Henley, Windsor & Marlow - BL to C77 2
Hereford to Newport D 54 8
Hertford and Hatfield - BLs around E 58 1 6
Hertford Loop E 71 0
Hexham to Carlisle D 75 3
Hitchin to Peterborough D 07 4
Holborn Viaduct to Lewisham A 81 9
Horsham - Branch Lines around A 02 4
Huntingdon - Branch Line to A 93 2

I
Ilford to Shenfield C 97 0
Ilfracombe - Branch Line to B 21 3
Industrial Rlys of the South East A 09 3
Ipswich to Saxmundham C 41 3
Isle of Wight Lines - 50 yrs C 12 3

K
Kent Narrow Gauge C 45 1
Kidderminster to Shrewsbury E 10 9
Kingsbridge - Branch Line to C 98 7
Kings Cross to Potters Bar E 62 8
Kingston & Hounslow Loops A 83 3
Kingswear - Branch Line to C 17 8

L
Lambourn - Branch Line to C 70 3
Launceston & Princetown - BL to C 19 2
Lewisham to Dartford A 92 5

Lines around Wimbledon B 75 6
Liverpool Street to Chingford D 01 2
Liverpool Street to Ilford C 34 5
Llandeilo to Swansea E 46 8
London Bridge to Addiscombe B 20 6
London Bridge to East Croydon A 58 1
Longmoor - Branch Lines to A 41 3
Looe - Branch Line to C 22 2
Lowestoft - Branch Lines around E 40 6
Ludlow to Hereford E 14 7
Lydney - Branch Lines around E 26 0
Lyme Regis - Branch Line to A 45 1
Lynton - Branch Line to B 04 6

M
Machynlleth to Barmouth E 54 3
March - Branch Lines around B 09 1
Marylebone to Rickmansworth D 49 4
Melton Constable to Yarmouth Beach E 03 1
Mexborough to Swinton E 36 9
Midhurst - Branch Lines around A 49 9
Mitcham Junction Lines B 01 5
Mitchell & company C 59 8
Monmouth - Branch Lines to E 20 8
Monmouthshire Eastern Valleys D 71 5
Moretonhampstead - BL to C 27 7
Moreton-in-Marsh to Worcester D 26 5
Mountain Ash to Neath D 80 7

N
Newbury to Westbury C 66 6
Newcastle to Hexham D 69 2
Newport (IOW) - Branch Lines to A 26 0
Newquay - Branch Lines to C 71 0
Newton Abbot to Plymouth C 60 4
Newtown to Aberystwyth E 41 3
North East German Narrow Gauge D 44 9
Northern France Narrow Gauge C 75 8
North London Line B 94 7
North Woolwich - BLs around C 65 9

O
Ongar - Branch Line to E 05 5
Oswestry - Branch Lines around E 60 4
Oxford to Bletchley D 57 9
Oxford to Moreton-in-Marsh D 15 9

P
Paddington to Ealing C 37 6
Paddington to Princes Risborough C 81 9
Padstow - Branch Line to B 54 1
Peterborough to Kings Lynn E 32 1
Plymouth - BLs around B 98 5
Plymouth to St. Austell C 63 5
Pontypool to Mountain Ash D 65 4
Porthmadog 1954-94 - BL around B 31 2
Portmadoc 1923-46 - BL around B 13 8
Portsmouth to Southampton A 31 4
Portugal Narrow Gauge E 67 3
Potters Bar to Cambridge D 70 8
Princes Risborough - Branch Lines to D 05 0
Princes Risborough to Banbury C 85 7

R
Reading to Basingstoke B 27 5
Reading to Didcot C 79 6
Reading to Guildford A 47 5
Redhill to Ashford A 73 4
Return to Blaenau 1970-82 C 64 2
Rhymney and New Tredegar Lines E 48 2
Rickmansworth to Aylesbury D 61 6
Romania & Bulgaria Narrow Gauge E 23 9
Romneyrail C 32 1
Ross-on-Wye - Branch Lines around E 30 7
Rugby to Birmingham E 37 6
Ryde to Ventnor A 19 2

S
Salisbury to Westbury B 39 8
Saxmundham to Yarmouth C 69 7
Saxony Narrow Gauge D 47 0
Seaton & Sidmouth - Branch Lines to A 95 6
Selsey - Branch Line to A 04 8
Sheerness - Branch Line to B 16 2

Shrewsbury - Branch Line to A 86 4
Shrewsbury to Chester E 70 3
Shrewsbury to Ludlow E 21 5
Shrewsbury to Newtown E 29 1
Sierra Leone Narrow Gauge D 28 9
Sirhowy Valley Line E 12 3
Sittingbourne to Ramsgate A 90 1
Slough to Newbury C 54 7
South African Two-foot gauge E 51 2
Southampton to Bournemouth A 42 0
Southern France Narrow Gauge C 47 5
South London Line B 46 6
Southwold - Branch Line to A 15 4
Spalding - Branch Lines around E 52 9
St Albans to Bedford D 08 1
St. Austell to Penzance C 67 3
Steaming through the Isle of Wight A 56 7
Steaming through West Hants A 69 7
Stourbridge to Wolverhampton E 16 1
St. Pancras to Barking D 68 5
St. Pancras to St. Albans C 78 9
Stratford-upon-Avon to Birmingham D 77 7
Stratford-upon-Avon to Cheltenham C 25 3
Surrey Narrow Gauge C 87 1
Sussex Narrow Gauge C 68 0
Swanley to Ashford B 45 9
Swansea to Carmarthen E 59 8
Swindon to Bristol C 96 3
Swindon to Gloucester D 46 3
Swindon to Newport D 30 2
Swiss Narrow Gauge C 94 9

T
Talyllyn - 50 years C 39 0
Taunton to Barnstaple B 60 2
Taunton to Exeter C 82 6
Tavistock to Plymouth B 88 6
Tenterden - Branch Line to A 21 5
Three Bridges to Brighton A 35 2
Tilbury Loop C 86 4
Tiverton - Branch Lines around C 62 8
Tivetshall to Beccles D 41 8
Tonbridge to Hastings A 44 4
Torrington - Branch Lines to B 37 4
Towcester - Branch Lines around E 39 0
Tunbridge Wells - Branch Lines to A 32 1

U
Upwell - Branch Line to B 64 0

V
Victoria to Bromley South A 98 7
Vivarais Revisited E 08 6

W
Wantage - Branch Line to D 25 8
Wareham to Swanage - 50 yrs D 09 8
Waterloo to Windsor A 54 3
Waterloo to Woking A 38 3
Watford to Leighton Buzzard D 45 6
Welshpool to Llanfair E 49 9
Wenford Bridge to Fowey C 09 3
Westbury to Bath B 55 8
Westbury to Taunton C 76 5
West Cornwall Mineral Railways D 48 7
West Croydon to Epsom B 08 4
West German Narrow Gauge D 93 7
West London - Branch Lines of C 50 5
West London Line B 84 8
West Wiltshire - Branch Lines of D 12 8
Weymouth - Branch Lines around A 65 9
Willesden Junction to Richmond B 71 8
Wimbledon to Beckenham C 58 1
Wimbledon to Epsom B 62 6
Wimborne - Branch Lines around A 97 0
Wisbech 1800-1901 C 93 2
Wisbech - Branch Lines around C 01 7
Woking to Alton A 59 8
Woking to Portsmouth A 25 3
Woking to Southampton A 55 0
Wolverhampton to Shrewsbury E 44 4
Worcester to Birmingham D 97 5
Worcester to Hereford D 38 8
Worthing to Chichester A 06 2

Y
Yeovil - 50 yrs change C 38 3
Yeovil to Dorchester A 76 5
Yeovil to Exeter A 91 8